Agroclimatic Atlas

of Ireland

James F. Collins
Thomas Cummins
Editors

ΛSΜЄⅭ

Dublin

Joint Working Group on Applied Agricultural Meteorology

1996

Previous AGMET publications

Climate, Weather and Irish Agriculture, edited by T. Keane, 1986.

Proceedings of Conference on Weather and Agriculture, edited by T. Keane, 1988.

Weather, Soils and Pollution from Agriculture, compiled by M. Sherwood, 1992.

The Future of Irish Agriculture—Role of Climate, edited by J.F. Collins, 1992, proceedings of a conference held at University College Dublin.

Irish Farming, Weather and Environment, edited by T. Keane, 1992.

The Balance of Water, edited by T. Keane and E. Daly, 1994, proceedings of a conference held at Trinity College Dublin.

Published 29–February, 1996 in Ireland
by the Joint Working Group on Applied Agricultural Meteorology
care of
Agriculture Building,
University College,
Belfield, Dublin 4,
Ireland

Design and Production Paul Callanan at DBA Publications.
Printed in Ireland by Prime Print.

ISBN 0 9511551 4 8

Contents

D. Definite   M. Maybe

Acknowledgements

AGMET wishes to thank the following for permission to include their material in this atlas

Academic Press	29b, 33, 37, 39, 153.
Ballykilcavan Press	31.
David and Charles	59b.
Economic and Social Research Institute	53.
Environmental Protection Agency	85, 87.
Forest Service, Dublin	59a.
Geography Publications	177.
Geological Survey of Ireland	29a.
Geological Survey of Ireland; K.T. Cullen & Co.	66, 67, 68, 179.
Hulton Educational Publications Ltd.	13.
Institute of Public Administration	33, 35.
International Hydrological Programme	75, 77, 79.
Irish Geography	61, 141.
Irish Journal of Agricultural Research	139b, 167, 181.
Longman	21, 23, 125, 135.
Meteorological Service, Dublin	71, 89, 91, 101, 109, 121, 137, 157.
Meteorological Service; P.K. Rohan	105, 111, 113, 115, 117, 127b, 129, 131, 133, 139b.
Methuen & Co.	25, 27a.
Ordnance Survey Office, Dublin	15, 17, 19, 93.
Oxford University Press	123.
Royal Dublin Society	57.
The Queen's University, Belfast	63, 175.
The Queen's University and University of Ulster	149, 155.
The Stationery Office, Dublin	171.
Teagasc, Dublin	27a, 41, 43, 45, 47, 49, 94, 95, 96, 147, 169, 181.
University College Dublin, Environmental Institute	103.
University College Dublin, FERG	83, 143, 185, 187.
University College Dublin, Remote Sensing Lab.	93.

Sponsors

The AGMET group wishes to thank the following for their generous sponsorship

Agricultural Trust Ltd.

B.A.S.F. Ireland Ltd.

Goulding Chemicals Ltd.

R&H Hall Ltd.

Coillte Teoranta

An Bord Glas

Fyffes Group Ireland Ltd.

Whelehan, T.P., Son & Co. Ltd.

Showerings (Irl.) Ltd.

Golden Vale Creameries plc.

If meteorology is the science of the atmosphere, then agrometeorology focuses that science and its findings on conditions at, near and below ground level. This is the place where plants and animals complete their life cycles, where thousands of day-to-day and hour-to-hour activities are pursued and where the foundations of our economy are anchored. Our climate then is one of our greatest natural resource assets, affecting as it does the way we manage our soils, the crops we grow and the animals we rear; it also has implications for other activities—how we manage our wastes, protect our water resources and indeed how we look after our own health and welfare. Agroclimatology is an activity aimed at putting the results of long term weather information and a range of data from a host of other scientific activities into a form that can be used by farmers and other land managers. Simply, it puts numbers on what weather means to people who work on the land.

The AGMET Group's full title is "Joint Working Group on Applied Agricultural Meteorology". It is a group of interested people, including members from the Meteorological Service, Teagasc (the agricultural advisory body), the Geological Survey of Ireland and the Office of Public Works as well as Universities and Colleges. Membership is open to all those interested in and willing to promote the uses of agrometeorology in Ireland.

The books, reports and conferences of AGMET are all attempts to bring the existing knowledge of agricultural meteorology to a wider audience. This atlas is the latest part of that effort.

The editors are members of the Faculty of Agriculture of University College Dublin. Jim Collins is a lecturer in the Department of Crop Science, Horticulture and Forestry, with primary and master's degrees from the National University of Ireland, and a Ph.D. from North Carolina State University. His major teaching and research activities are in the field of soil science. Thomas Cummins has a degree in forestry from University College Dublin, and is a researcher with the Forest Ecosystem Research Group of the Department of Environmental Resource Management. His main area of research is in measuring atmospheric deposition and its effects on soils and water.

Many Generations of Men are come and gone from this Earth, since the Formation of Adam *out of it, yet the Earth it self with its verdant Furniture abideth for ever.*

And by the Almighty Creator's Word Grass groweth for the Cattle, and Herb for the Service of Man, for he bringeth forth Food out of the Earth, even Wine to recruit the Strength, and ease the Cares of Mortals, Oils and Balsams for Perfumes, and that Staff of Bread upon which the Prince and Peasant must lean themselves.

So that although we are not the same Nation of Men, who dwelt here a thousand Years ago, yet the spontaneous Plants are the same they were in the time of the Danes *and* Bryan Boro, *and in my Opinion it had been more Benefit to Mankind to have made stricter Inquiries into the natural Growth of the Soil; (the Beauty of which whilst it allures our Eyes, and even captivates our Senses, raises in us the most exalted Idea of the Magnificence of the great Creator) than to have trifled away Pains and Time, in amusing us with fabulous Stories concerning the Generations of Men preceding us, whose almost endless Genealogies are often fallacious and dubious, and where they are certain, of very little Importance to us in civil Affairs, not that I blame laudable Searches into Antiquity, but I give the preference to those durable and succouring Studies.*

Having for several Years diverted my self both here, and in the North of England, *in the Contemplation of Vegetables, (My Inclination leading me to the Botanick Studies) I have at last ventured to publish this Essay, which has cost me some Pains, proposing thereby to stir up others of a better Genius, and more Leisure to Emulation: For it is not so much to please my own Fancy with the vain Conceit of being an Author, that I compiled this small Work, as with a Design to assist miserable Mortals of the same reasonable Species with my self, that they might live in Plenty and Ease, while they sojourn here on Earth; what Tendency there is in this Collection for such an End, I freely submit to the Opinion of better Judges.*

Caleb Threlkeld
Synopsis Stirpium Hibernicarum
Dublin, 1726

Where maps are involved, the well-used proverb about a picture being worth a thousand words is surely apt. Well-made maps place a vast amount of information before the reader in a highly visible form. They are therefore amongst the educator's most valuable tools.

Since its inception in 1984, the Joint Working Group on Applied Agricultural Meteorology (AGMET) has been aware that a great amount of information pertaining to Irish agricultural climatology was stored in map form, much of it not readily available to its members, or the interested public. It was also aware that much of this information incorporated a wide range of interrelated disciplines whose common bond was agroclimatic.

Following its 1992 Conference the AGMET Group assumed the task of assembling the most salient parts of published agroclimatic information into a single volume. It had the unenviable job of selecting only a fraction of what was previously published in books, journals, reports, bulletins, proceedings and other media. In many instances only one or two examples from a whole series of maps could be included. While preference was given to maps which could be republished at their original scale, the editors used some portions of larger scale maps to illustrate what was already published. The inclusion of "dated" maps was justified in several instances to indicate changing circumstances.

Opinions and comments in the text are those of the editors and not those of the makers of the original maps. The editors wish to thank all those who helped to put the collection together; they got unstinting support from other members of the Atlas Subgroup within AGMET (listed below) as well as cooperation from a wide variety of individuals. They wish to acknowledge especially those publishing houses who gave permission to republish, and the sponsors whose financial support made the whole effort feasible.

AGMET Atlas Subgroup

J.F. Collins, University College Dublin, convenor
T. Cummins, University College Dublin
E. Daly, Eugene Daly Associates, formerly Geological Survey of Ireland
S. Diamond, Teagasc, Johnstown Castle, Wexford
T. Keane, Meteorological Service, Glasnevin, Dublin
M. McEntee, St. Mary's College of Education, Belfast
M. Walsh, Teagasc, Athenry, Co. Galway

The maritime climate of Ireland is explained as the product of its location as an island on the eastern side of an ocean in mid latitudes. This explanation is illustrated by a variety of maps which show the dominance of westerly air masses following oceanic tracks and frequently supplemented by weather systems incorporating warm and cold maritime air. These atmospheric factors are altered by the North Atlantic Drift, an influence clearly revealed in winter sea temperatures, while net radiation provides a measure of the significance of Ireland's latitudinal position.

These geographical facts determine the well known characteristics of the Irish climate: cool summers, mild winters, no marked seasonality, high amounts of cloud, high atmospheric humidities, frequent wet days, windiness, evaporation exceeding rainfall for a short period each year, and the impression of coolness these combine to give.

However, this Atlas stresses the variation in climate on the island, a fact easily overlooked when confronted by the reality of the cliché that there is no Irish climate, only weather. Implicit in the maps of this atlas is that there are significant environmental gradients creating more than one climate in Ireland. Chief among these is the change with altitude, explained by the frequency of polar air with steep lapse rates and high humidities. Thus a rise of 150 m in Kerry is equivalent to a move northwards to Sligo at sea level when growing conditions are considered. Also important is location relative to the main tracks of depressions. There is a drop in the annual mean atmospheric pressure from over 1014 hPa in the south and southeast to 1012 hPa in Donegal showing low pressure systems are more common towards the northwest. This gradient is more graphically expressed by facts such as: there are more than twice as many days with gales at Malin Head than at Rosslare. Of lesser importance but locally significant are nearness to the coast or large lakes, soil types, topography including aspect and urbanisation. Hence we have longer growing seasons in areas such as north County Dublin or the Ards peninsula than adjacent inland areas. Even lakes such as Lough Neagh and Lower Lough Erne have discernible influences on temperatures. Similarly, meteorological stations in peatland can be separated from neighbouring mineral soil stations by parameters such as frost frequency, while cold air draining from surrounding high ground helps explain greater frost frequency in low-lying inland areas such as Kilkenny. Also Dublin and Belfast have distinct heat islands.

These climatic gradients operate in the context of pedological, geological and topographic differences. If we hope to understand the processes and origins of the Irish landscape, whether as agriculturists or geographers or other natural scientists, then the information in this atlas is invaluable. If in free market conditions we have to depend solely on our own resources, then the interactions and interrelationships between our soils, waters, air, fauna and flora, and the modulating influences of our climate, as recorded in this volume, will take on a new and added significance. The atlas should also help historians and prehistorians understand the stage on which human events take place.

The maps opposite show the relative positions of airmasses and fronts in both January and July for northwestern Europe.

Interpreting the Maps

The maps in this atlas are from a wide variety of sources, and reflect the needs and intentions of the various authors within the original publications. The preparation of this collection has not involved significant editing or updating of maps, serving rather to guide the reader towards the range of existing productions than to present a wholly new compilation.

The text accompanying the maps aims to explain the values presented, and the use for which the map was intended. This text is not derived from the original publications, and does not necessarily reflect the opinions of the original authors of the maps. The footnotes give the original publication, and/or other sources of similar information which may be more easily available.

The precision implied by line widths, point sizes and other graphical tools must be carefully interpreted. Where a cartographer decides to place a line may represent the mean location of an irregularly varying value, or the middle of a zone of continuous change, or a fair guess at where the line should go. When information has been available as to the number of data points or the period of observation, this has been given, and is the best guide to the reliability of the map. Similarly, the information at the time the maps were produced may no longer be accurate in some cases. This collection is intended to bring a wide variety of existing maps to a larger audience, and not to update the considerable body of work drawn on.

Church, R.J.H., Hall, P., Lawrence, G.R.P., Mead, W.R. and Mutton, A., 1973. An Advanced Geography of Northern and Western Europe. 2nd edition, Hulton Educational Publications Ltd., Amersham, England.

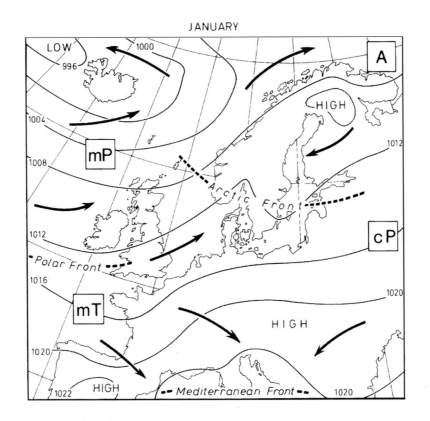

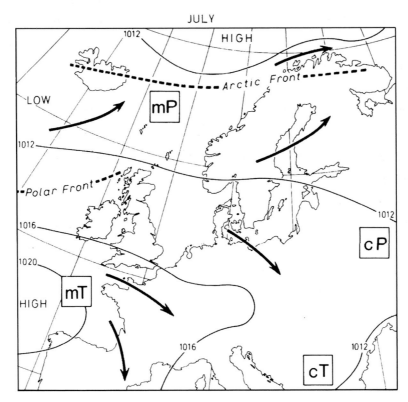

Mean positions of airmasses and fronts in January and July, northwestern Europe; arrows show generalised circulation. Principal airmasses are as follows: mP: maritime polar; A: arctic; cP: continental polar; mT: maritime tropical; cT: continental tropical

Ordnance Survey maps

Most countries, Ireland included, have long histories of land surveying and map making. Early attempts were the result of exploration; later ones were commissioned for the purposes of warfare, conquest and the sub-divisions of conquered lands. Further refinements were brought on by the requirements of legal ownership, road making and taxation; hence ground measurement and cartographic accuracy made maps progressively more reliable.

Beaufort, Petty, Scalé, Rocque, Speed, Taylor and Vallancy were all famous map makers, but private mapmaking went into decline when the government established a branch of the Ordnance Survey in the Phoenix Park, Dublin in 1824. It was given the task of establishing an accurate trigonometric foundation for all mapmaking and of delimiting the country's 62,000 townlands as well as villages, towns, altitudes and most major permanent features of the landscape. By 1846 it had produced a "set of some 1,900 austerely beautiful six-inch engravings" of the whole country—a feat not accomplished at that scale anywhere else in the world at that time. In subsequent decades the Ordnance Survey augmented its collection to include maps at larger scales (25-inch to the mile of intensively used land, 50-inch and 60-inch of various towns) and of reduced scale (1-inch, half-inch and quarter-inch to the mile) more suited to scientific, demographic, touristic and administrative uses. Progress in this century has included updating, resurveying (especially in the vicinity of towns and cities), adoption of a national grid, use of colour printing and in recent decades, the use of metric scales.

This map is an index of the 1:50,000 scale (2 cm to 1 km) "Discovery" series of maps, which will be completed in the late 1990s. This series involves a completely new mapping of contours, at 10 m height intervals, based on recent aerial photography. Some areas will also have maps prepared at 1:25,000 scale.

Ordnance Survey of Ireland, Phoenix Park, Dublin.
Andrews, J.S., 1978. Irish Maps: Irish Heritage Series No. 18. Eason and Son, Dublin.

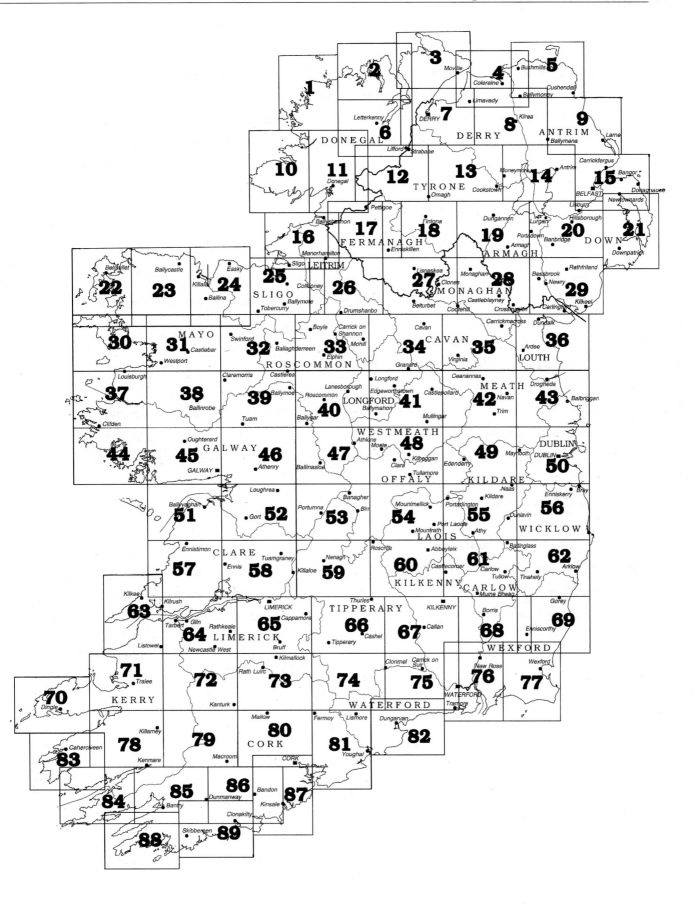

Index to the 1:50,000 scale Ordnance Survey Discovery Series maps in preparation

The six-inch maps

Maps at a scale of 6 inches to 1 mile (1:10,560) show a wealth of information. The more complex the area depicted on them, the more detail is shown on the maps. They record the positions of places and things with respect to one another and, where appropriate, their names. Included are modes of communication such as roads, railways and streets, physical features such as hills and streams, field boundaries, buildings, earthworks, contour lines and spot heights. A standard system of symbols is used, making it easy for the user to read the map. This map is an example of a very rural area; we can learn a lot about it from this small sample.

The contrast between the bottom right (southeast) and top left (northwest) corners of this extract lies in the presence and absence of enclosed land, the altitude as shown by the 100 foot contour lines and the use of map symbols to indicate rock outcrop, marshy meadow and hummocky terrain. The map also shows:

— the location of main and minor roads, the village with its public buildings (chapel, school, barracks, post office);
— townland names and their extent (eg. Kealkill occupies 776 acres, 1 rood and 21 perches); drainage (large stream near top left and top right corners), as well as a ruined castle, fords, waterfalls and a modern bridge;
— field shapes and sizes reflecting various stages of enclosure accommodating the topography and soil conditions;
— grid references at the corners and the scale in bar form.

Townland boundaries are shown by a dotted line, usually along a fence line or in the bed of a river; contour lines by dotted line (dots very close together) and the altitude given in feet above sea level; field boundaries by solid lines; unfenced roads and lanes by sets of parallel dashed lines. Numbers along the main road are spot altitudes, while those with a decimal number and "BM" indicate the exact height of a mark (known as a bench mark, and looking like a bird's footprint) carved in stone on a permanent structure, in feet above ordnance datum (an altitude standard related to sea level).

Apart from a map such as this being used as a legal document to show the location and extent of a holding, the six-inch maps have been extremely useful in a range of areas—in agriculture, forestry, environment, geography and many others.

Sample 1:10,560 scale map, showing an area at Kealkill, near Bantry, Co. Cork

Ordnance Survey of Ireland, Phoenix Park, Dublin.

DESCRIPTION

Map Scales

6inch
CK092   CK106

An tSuirbhéireacht Ordanáis,
Páirc an Fhionnuisce,
Baile Átha Cliath,
a thiomsaigh, a chóigh
agus a d'fhoilsigh.

Compiled, Printed and
Published at the Ordnance
Survey, Phoenix Park,
Dublin.

ORDNANCE SURVEY COMPOSITE MAP

Surveyed 1842
Revised 1898 – 1899
Levelled 0

Plot Ref. No. 0
Plot Date 25–OCT–1995

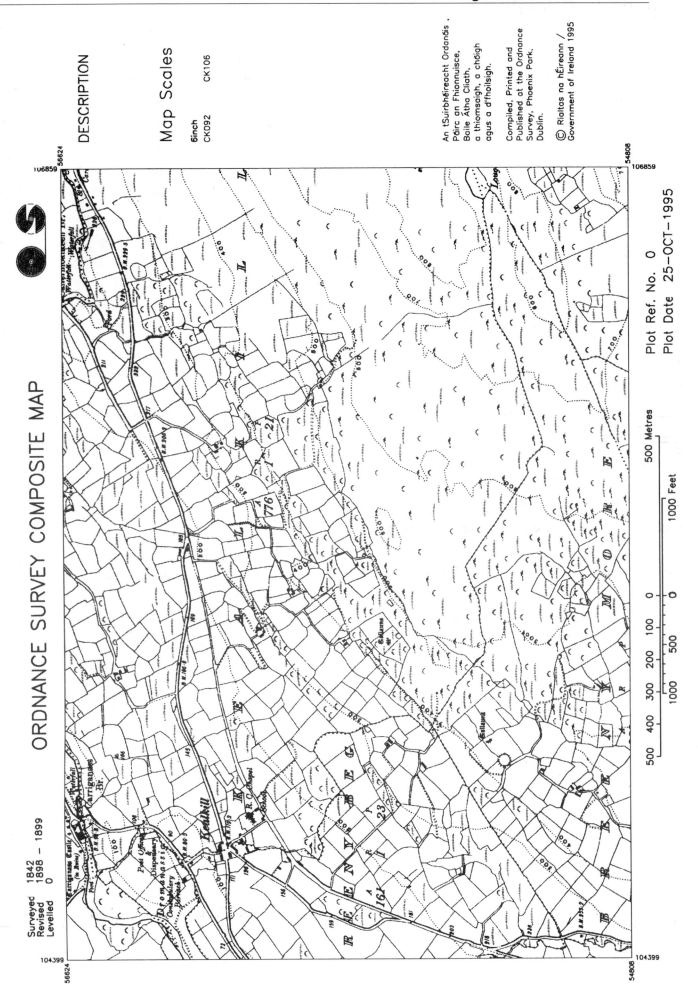

The 25-inch maps

While the six-inch maps were produced at exactly 6 inches to 1 mile or a scale ratio of 1 to 10,560, the twenty-five-inch maps were drawn at a scale of 1:2500 which is not exactly 25 inches to the mile (which would be 1:2534.1). However they are known informally as the 25-inch series. This is a sample of such a map from a location in Co. Cavan. It gives much of the information recorded in the 6-inch series. (townland and other names, rivers, buildings), but in greater detail. In this sample we can study the shapes and arrangements of fields, the shapes and layout of roads and the position of buildings relative to means of transport (roads) and power (eg. mills by the river). The impression is of a functional landscape with rectilinear fields of fairly uniform size (except near buildings). The ornamentation in the southwest and northeast corners reflects less intensive or non-farming use of land—the former having groves of decidu-ous trees beside the river and the latter having rough pasture and a non-permanent fence indicated by a dotted line.

The number printed in the centre of each field is the acreage to the third decimal place; chain symbols linking small plots to larger fields indicate that the areas of the enclosures are given together. The numbers along the diagonal main road are Ordnance Datum heights, with a benchmark (BM 370.8) indicated at the site of a house. The num-bers at the corners are grid reference numbers—those along the bottom and top are "eastings" and those on the left and right are "northings". These are given in metres. The southwest corner is 260.626 km east and 287.586 km north of the "false origin" (the lower left-hand corner) of the Irish National Grid. The north point need not always be shown on maps as it may be assumed that the top edge of the map sheet is to north.

Maps such as this are in regular use by farmers, advisers, local authorities and government officials and other bodies who deal with land and property.

Part of a Co. Cavan map at 1: 2500 scale ("25-inch")

Ordnance Survey of Ireland, Phoenix Park, Dublin.

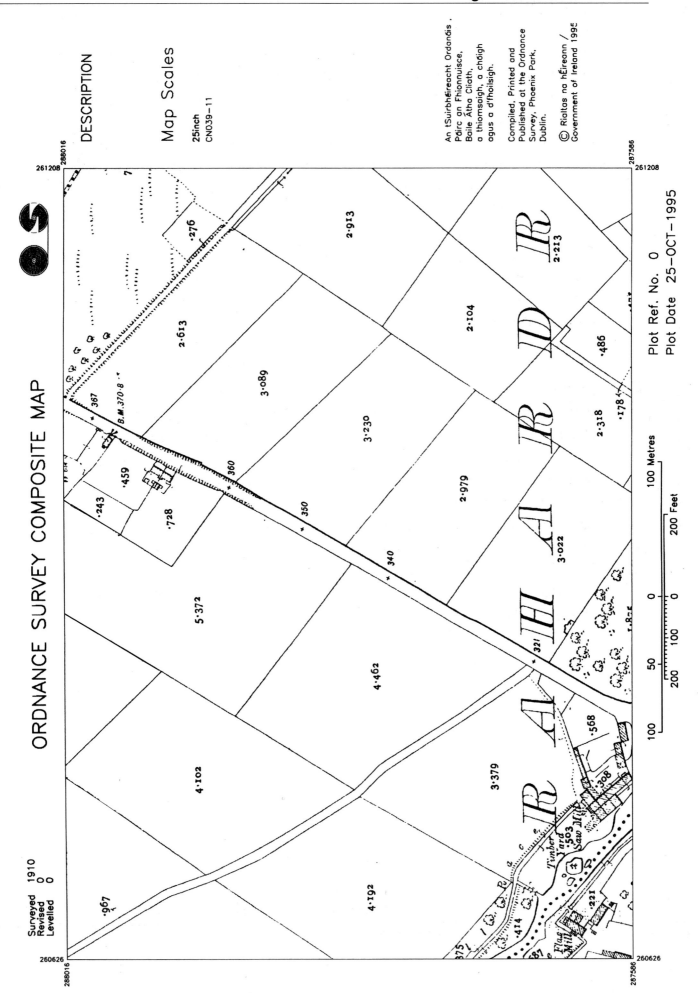

ORDNANCE SURVEY COMPOSITE MAP

DESCRIPTION

Map Scales

25inch
CN039–11

An tSuirbhéireacht Ordanáis.
Páirc an Fhionnuisce,
Baile Átha Cliath,
a thiomsaigh, a chóigh
agus a d'fhoilsigh.

Compiled, Printed and
Published at the Ordnance
Survey, Phoenix Park,
Dublin.

© Rialtas na hÉireann /
Government of Ireland 1995

Plot Ref. No. 0
Plot Date 25–OCT–1995

Surveyed 1910
Revised 0
Levelled 0

100 Metres

200 Feet

A view of Ireland

Even though it is an island in the Atlantic, Ireland may be regarded as a western extremity of a large geographic and geomorphic unit stretching eastwards as far as the Ural mountains—the Northern European Plain. It is justifiably part of a plain, since only a small part of the Irish landscape rises above about 200 m (656 feet) and the gradients of much of the midlands are less than 1-in-50. The country acquired its vertical and lateral profiles (relief and coastline) at various stages throughout geologic history, and indeed continues to change shape and form, however imperceptibly. The glacial processes of the Pleistocene era, including the fluctuations in sea-level with respect to land have been responsible for most of the finishing touches applied to the geologic structure. However, other climatically-driven processes (fluvial, aeolian, marine) continue to etch and mould the physical landscape. Similarly many aspects of our climate (rainfall, evapotranspiration, relative humidity, temperature, wind) dictate the nature of our soils, vegetative cover, and the purposes for which they have been, and are being, used.

Apart from showing the counties and the 200 m contour, this map depicts a very generalised boundary between "the physically better-endowed lands of the south and east" and "the physically harsher country to the north and west". This broad southeast-northwest pattern is explained and developed more fully in the maps that follow.

Orme, A.R., 1970. The World's Landscapes 4 Ireland. Longman, London.

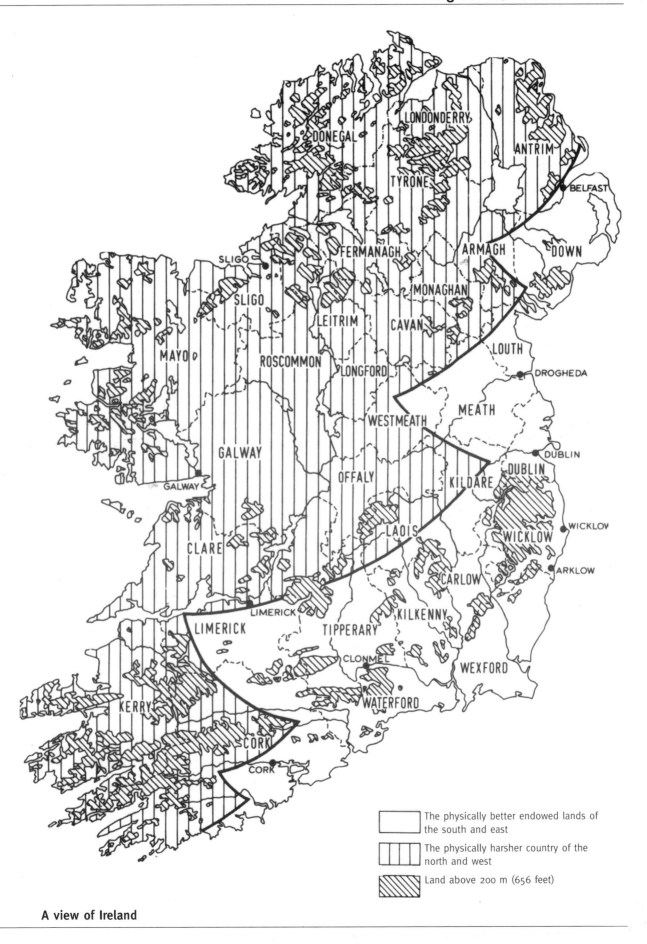

DONEGAL
LONDONDERRY
ANTRIM
TYRONE
BELFAST
FERMANAGH
ARMAGH
DOWN
SLIGO
MONAGHAN
SLIGO
LEITRIM
CAVAN
LOUTH
MAYO
ROSCOMMON
LONGFORD
DROGHEDA
MEATH
WESTMEATH
GALWAY
OFFALY
DUBLIN
DUBLIN
KILDARE
GALWAY
LAOIS
WICKLOW
WICKLOW
CLARE
ARKLOW
CARLOW
LIMERICK
KILKENNY
LIMERICK
TIPPERARY
LIMERICK
CLONMEL
WEXFORD
KERRY
WATERFORD
CORK
CORK

	The physically better endowed lands of the south and east
	The physically harsher country of the north and west
	Land above 200 m (656 feet)

A view of Ireland

Physical features

Long before agriculture and climate became subjects of scientific study, knowledge of the physical features of the country was a means of ensuring a livelihood. From the outset the rivers, lakes and estuaries were sources of food and corridors of transport, while the lowlands behind them were exploited for their plants and animals and materials for shelter. Lakes have often been used as habitation sites, while hills and ridge tops provided ceremonial, defensive or burial sites. Gradually the lowlands became populated; the high mountains and deep bogs were avoided on account of their low productive capacity and harsh climates.

Before climatic data was assembled it was possible to make judgements and decisions based on physical features. It was clear that conditions deteriorated on climbing a hill (the words 'climate' and 'climb' came from the same root).

A map of physical features of a country can help one predict a lot about climate and agriculture. By comparing it with other maps in this collection, many parallels can be seen, especially the occurrence of higher rainfall in the more mountainous areas. The contrast between mountainous, upland areas and the lowlands partly reflects the climates of the distant past and the role of weathering and erosion.

The fact that much of the land of Ireland is below 200 m has implications for runoff, soil development and land use. Topography also had a bearing on the location of inland synoptic weather stations and influences the interpretation of the data collected at these stations, and the interpolation of the data for places in between.

Orme, A.R., 1970. The World's Landscapes 4 Ireland. Longman, London.

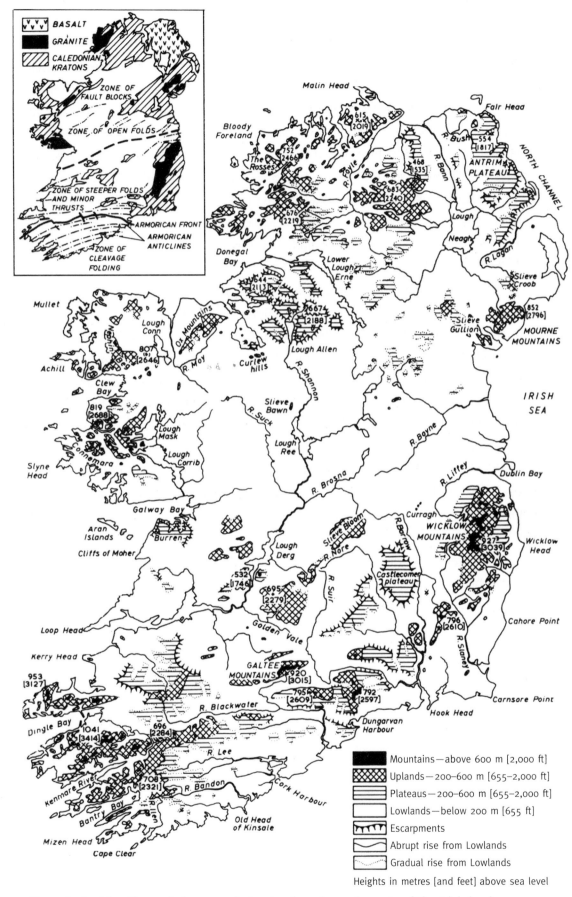

The principal landform, drainage and structural geology elements of the Irish landscape

Geomorphic regions

At its simplest, the geomorphic features of Ireland consist of two major components—a coastal mountainous rim surrounding a central plain. This map, however, gives a much more detailed and instructive view of the physical face of this island. It is immediately obvious that the Central Lowland (1) occupies over a third of the island. Most of it is developed on soluble limestone rock, studded with lake basins, some large, some small and many filled with peat. It is drained in all directions even though the Shannon receives the greatest share. The Leinster Axis (2) is dominated by granite mountains which stretch 110 km from Dublin to Waterford with less hilly and undulating terrain to the east and west. The Ridge-and-Valley province of Munster (3) is a large corrugated sheet of contrasting rocks with an east-west orientation, and rises to over 900 m in Kerry.

Of the remaining sixteen regions, five consist of fragmented uplands (4, 10, 12, 15 & 19) and five form plateaux with discontinuous outward-facing scarps (5, 6, 8, 14 & 17). Contrary to general belief much of west Co. Galway (9) is a lowland, "with kilometre after kilometre of sodden blanket bog littered with innumerable sheets of brown, peat-stained water". Two other coastal lowlands (7 & 13) could be regarded as severed pieces of the Central Lowland. Regions 16 (The Mid-Ulster Highlands) and 17 (The Basaltic Plateau) are very much opposites; the former has a central core of diverse rocks, the latter a central depression occupied by Lough Neagh. Most of the coastline of the former is a substantial retreating shoreline of shingle and sand; the latter proudly boasts of its magnificent basalt columns and rare mixture of tropically weathered interbasaltic beds and white flinty chalks.

The Cavan-Down Hill Country (18) is our equivalent of the Southern Uplands of Scotland, but is better known for its variety of rocks than for its scattering of low hills.

Herries Davies, G.L. and Stephens, N., 1978. The Geomorphology of the British Isles: Ireland. Methuen, London.

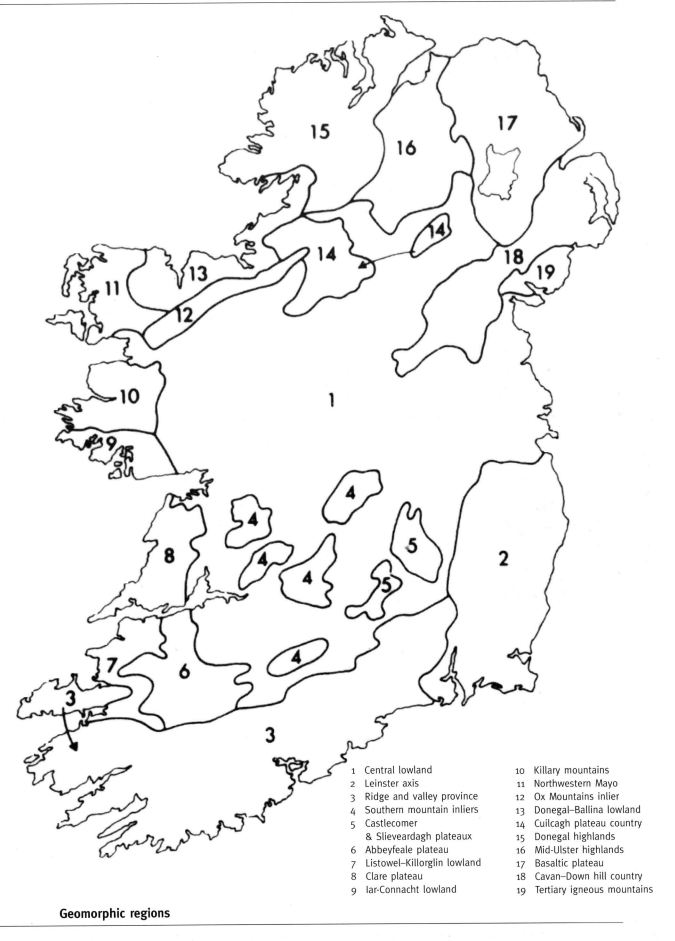

1 Central lowland
2 Leinster axis
3 Ridge and valley province
4 Southern mountain inliers
5 Castlecomer
   & Slieveardagh plateaux
6 Abbeyfeale plateau
7 Listowel–Killorglin lowland
8 Clare plateau
9 Iar-Connacht lowland

10 Killary mountains
11 Northwestern Mayo
12 Ox Mountains inlier
13 Donegal–Ballina lowland
14 Cuilcagh plateau country
15 Donegal highlands
16 Mid-Ulster highlands
17 Basaltic plateau
18 Cavan–Down hill country
19 Tertiary igneous mountains

Geomorphic regions

The maps facing are simplified maps of the geological floor of this country; that on the left has seven groups based on the physical characteristics of the rock, while than on the right has eleven (with notes) relating to the age and origin of the structures. The fact that about 50% of the country is floored by limestone (rare in the world scale) is counterbalanced by the complexity of the remaining 50%. The rock type has implications for climate (orogenic rain, fog, temperature lags), water resources (aquifers), topography (runoff, flood hazard), soil resources and land use (fertility, drainage). It is to be emphasised that small-scale maps like these hide the fact that there are many kinds of limestone, many forms of sandstone, many ages of shale and so on. The fact that the dominant rocks in south Cork are labelled 'Shale and Sandstone' in one map and 'Lower Carboniferous' in the other is not to be taken as an error. The former is more informative to those interested in the properties of rocks such as porosity, water transmission, and likely soil products; the latter helps our understanding of historical geology, age of the world, development of life-forms and a multitude of processes operating within the lithosphere.

Plate 4 shows the geology of Ireland in greater detail.

Gardiner, M.J. and Radford, T., 1980. Soil Associations of Ireland and Their Land Use Potential. Soil Survey Bulletin No. 36, An Foras Talúntais, Dublin.

Herries Davies, G.L. and Stephens, N., 1978. The Geomorphology of the British Isles Ireland. Methuen, London.

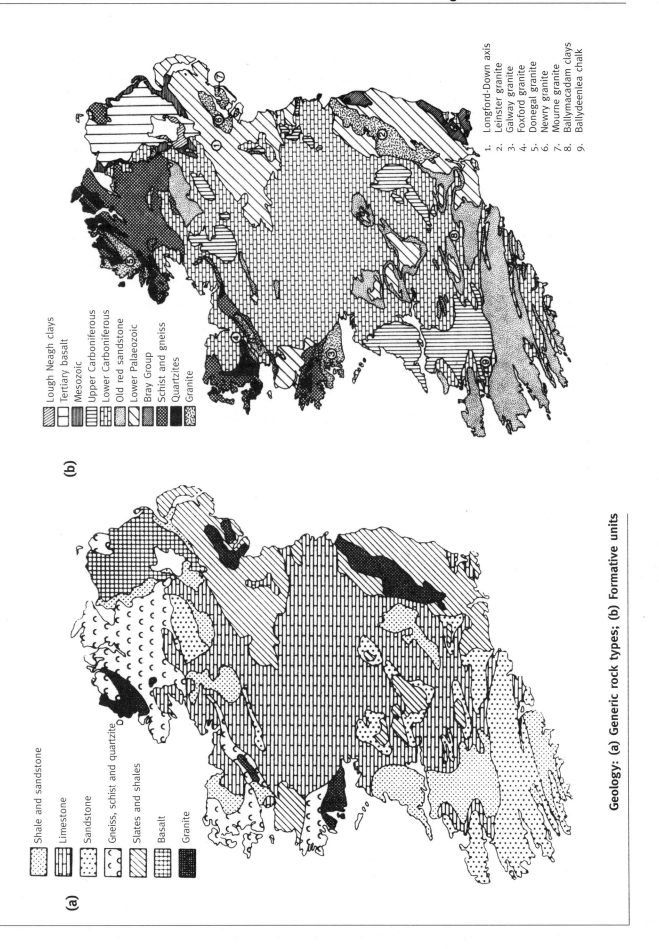

(b)

Lough Neagh clays
Tertiary basalt
Mesozoic
Upper Carboniferous
Lower Carboniferous
Old red sandstone
Lower Palaeozoic
Bray Group
Schist and gneiss
Quartzites
Granite

1. Longford-Down axis
2. Leinster granite
3. Galway granite
4. Foxford granite
5. Donegal granite
6. Newry granite
7. Mourne granite
8. Ballymacadam clays
9. Ballydeenlea chalk

(a)

Shale and sandstone
Limestone
Sandstone
Gneiss, schist and quartzite
Slates and shales
Basalt
Granite

Geology: (a) Generic rock types; (b) Formative units

Glacial geomorphology

Several words of Gaelic origin have found their place in the language of geomorphologists: drumlin: from *drum*, a hill, ridge, and *in*, the diminutive form; esker: from *eiscir*, a gravelly ridge; kame: from *cam*, crooked, suggesting undulating terrain. These and many other features are legacies of a period of about two million years when temperatures oscillated many times and when ice cover waxed and waned, leaving behind it a new, fresh landscape in which much of our present day fauna and flora was established and in which our soils and agriculture developed.

There is direct evidence of no more than two glaciations in Ireland, and of the two, most of the depositional and erosional features belong to the last one (known as the Weichselian in continental Europe or the Fenitian (formerly Midlandian) here. Map (a) shows the location of the major areas of ice accumulation during the Fenitian, with three major domes "on land" and coalescing with Scottish ice in the Irish Sea Basin.

The major legacies of the glacial epoch are depicted in map (b). Numbers 1 to 12 indicate various stages of deglaciation evidenced on the ground by large series of deposits (moraines). Drumlins are a distinct form of ground moraine—till moulded into repeating hills by advancing ice—while most of the unshaded area is covered with till in less-organised ground moraines. The letters OD (older drift) refer to the earlier belief that the areas in question did not undergo glaciation during the last, Fenitian, stage, but were subjected to periglacial activity, resulting in many phenomena associated with permafrost and freezing conditions.

Warren, W.P., 1993. Wicklow in the Ice Age an Introduction and Guide to the Glacial Geology of the Wicklow District. Geological Survey of Ireland, Dublin.
Mc Cabe, A.M., 1985 (after Synge, 1969). Glacial Geomorphology. Chapter 4 in: The Quaternary History of Ireland, edited by K.J. Edwards and W.P. Warren. Academic Press, London.
Synge, F.M., 1969. In: Quaternary Geology and Climate. National Academy of Sciences, Washington, D.C.

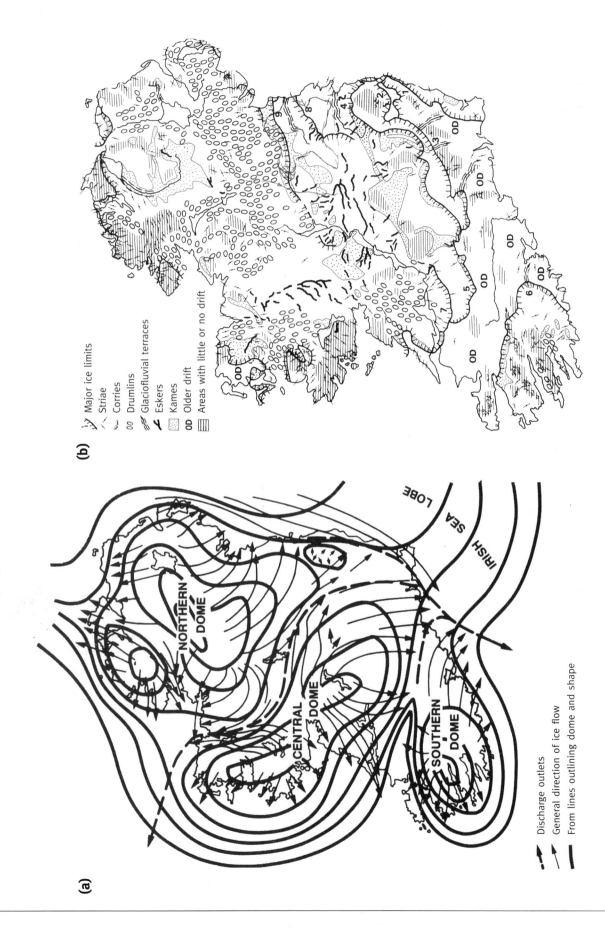

(b)

Major ice limits
Striae
Corries
Drumlins
Glaciofluvial terraces
Eskers
Kames
OD Older drift
Areas with little or no drift

(a)

Discharge outlets
General direction of ice flow
From lines outlining dome and shape

Glacial geomorphology: (a) General pattern of glaciation during the most recent (Fenitian) stage; (b) Glacial and fluvioglacial features

Quaternary geology of Co. Laois

The Quaternary geology map of Co. Laois is used as an example of the complexity of the glacial landscape at county level. Apart from the many glacial features shown, the fact that seven different solid (bedrock) rocks are indicated shows that the glacial cover is very variable, and that the contributors to glacial deposits are quite contrasting. The presence of erratics of Galway granite on the northwest slopes of the Slieve Bloom mountains is an indication of the distance glaciers may travel. Included in the list of glacial features are those laid down by advancing ice and those associated with deglaciation and meltwaters.

The hummocky drift is an unsorted and unstratified mixture of material downloaded from the ice, generally loamy in texture, but fine textured where finely ground rock flour predominated. Outwash sand and gravel resulted from transport by meltwater within the ice or from the ice face. Where this material was enclosed in ice tunnels it formed long sinuous ridges (eskers) of which the Timahoe and Portlaoise ones are well known. Morainic ridges are associated with a waxing ice front and a kame-and-kettle topography. Striae and meltwater channels represent the extremes of ice erosional features, the former being tiny etchings and grooves in the bedrock which are useful in indicating directions of ice movement; meltwater channels, on the other hand are deep, steep-sided gashes in the landscape made over decades if not centuries of rapidly escaping water on its way to the sea.

While more recent in age, raised bogs and alluvium may be regarded as part of Quaternary heritage, even though the geological nature of the former may be disputed.

Feehan, J., 1983. Laois an Environmental History. Ballykilcavan Press, Stradbally, Co. Laois.

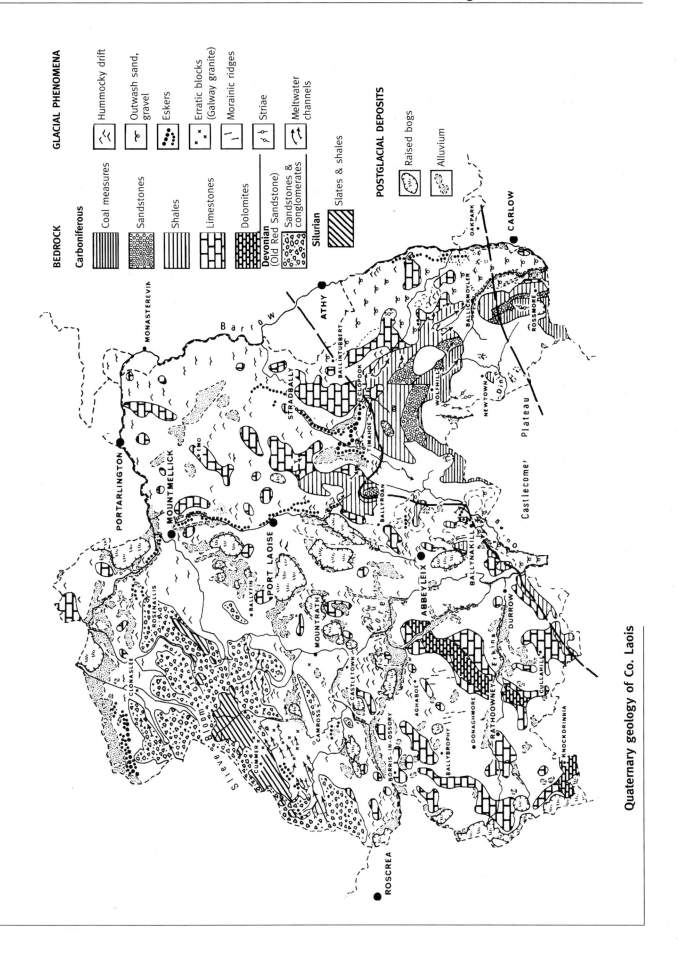

BEDROCK

Carboniferous

▥	Coal measures
⣿	Sandstones
▥	Shales
▦	Limestones
▦	Dolomites

Devonian
(Old Red Sandstone)

⣿	Sandstones & conglomerates

Silurian

▨	Slates & shales

GLACIAL PHENOMENA

⌃⌃	Hummocky drift
⸦	Outwash sand, gravel
••	Eskers
××	Erratic blocks (Galway granite)
/	Morainic ridges
⸜⸝	Striae
↰↱	Meltwater channels

POSTGLACIAL DEPOSITS

⬚	Raised bogs
⬚	Alluvium

Quaternary geology of Co. Laois

Glacial features of Sligo Bay

It may be a consolation to some in this era of predicted global warming and sea level rise that part of this island is rising out of the sea, albeit at an extremely slow rate. The reason for this rise is a release from the downwarping of the earth's crust following the enormous weight of glacial ice which was present for the best part of the last two million years. Evidence for this readjustment (isostatic) is common along our coast, especially in the northern half; but it is accompanied by other evidence—that of an absolute change (eustatic) resulting from the lowering and rising of sea levels globally as a result of converting vast amounts of water to ice and vice versa during the ice age. Both changes may be complimentary or balancing and evidence for both often lie side by side in parts of our coastline.

This map of the Knocknarea part of Co. Sligo is included to show details of glacial legacies, both constructional (beaches, eskers, drumlins) and erosional (scarps, meltwater channels) as well as the common occurrence of marine features in both Sligo and Ballisodare Bays. There are remains of former beaches at three levels in Sligo Bay (6-7 m, 5-6 m and at 3 m above mean sea level). Each is dominated by shells of oyster species and some have charcoal layers, which indicate habitation of those areas by mesolithic peoples. In more recent times these shelly layers have been exploited as a source of lime for agricultural purposes.

Synge, F.M., 1985. Coastal Evolution. Chapter 6 in: The Quaternary History of Ireland, edited by K.J. Edwards and W.P. Warren. Academic Press, London.

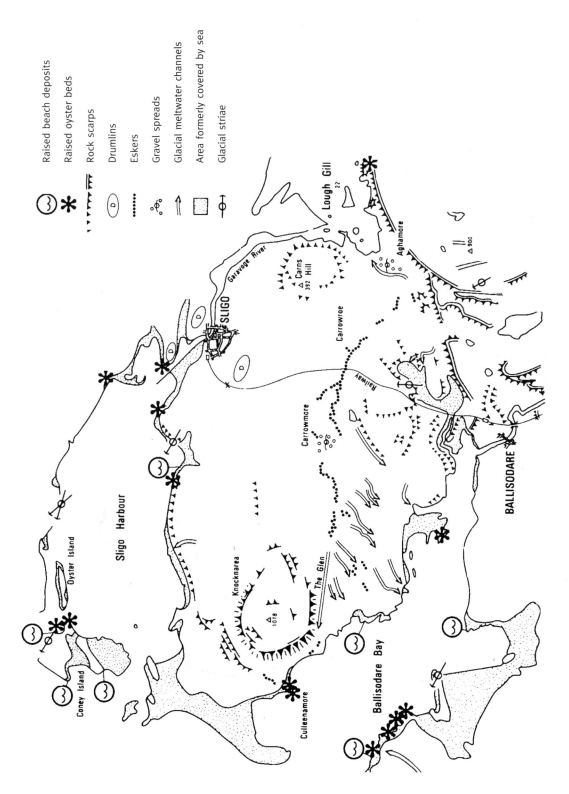

Legend:

-) Raised beach deposits
- * Raised oyster beds
- Rock scarps
- Drumlins
- Eskers
- Gravel spreads
- Glacial meltwater channels
- Area formerly covered by sea
- Glacial striae

Lough Gill

22'

Aghamore

△ 900

Garavogue River

△ Carns
392 Hill

SLIGO

Carrowroe

Railway

Carrowmore

Sligo Harbour

Oyster Island

Knocknarea

The Glen

△ 1078

Coney Island

Culleenamore

Ballisodare Bay

BALLISODARE

Glacial features around Sligo and Ballisodare Bays

Rock aquifers

It is common knowledge that our rivers keep flowing and our wells producing water long after the rain stops. The reason is simple: most rocks have pores/fractures to some degree and these pores/fractures hold water. The nearer the surface and the more weathered and faulted rocks are, the greater their porosity and permeability. The term aquifer refers to rocks or sediments of which all or part is saturated with water and is capable of yielding or supplying significant quantities of water. However, rocks vary enormously in their ability to hold and transmit water. This map shows that some of the limestone rocks have extensive aquifers unlike the older Ordovician shales and Devonian sandstones which do not hold or transmit large quantities of water. In general the older rocks are less porous and most of our granites, bedded limestones, some of the sandstones and shales are virtually impermeable (put another way, only the impermeable rocks have resisted weathering for such long periods). The productivity of the limestones is very variable in places due to secondary fissuring and joints. Local areas with fissured volcanic beds (Co. Waterford) and relatively recent sandstones (Co. Monaghan) have high-yielding aquifers. Limestones provide most dependable water yields where the flow is structurally controlled as in the E-W valleys of Munster. The very low summer flow in some of the rivers around the head of Galway Bay is an indication of poor reserves in the rock and the likelihood of rapid run-off in winter.

Plate 2 is an aquifer map and Plate 3 is a map of the vulnerability of those aquifers to water pollution, both presented in colour.

Drew, D.P., 1979. Water. Chapter 3 in: Irish Resources and Land Use, edited by D.A. Gillmor. Institute of Public Administration, Dublin.

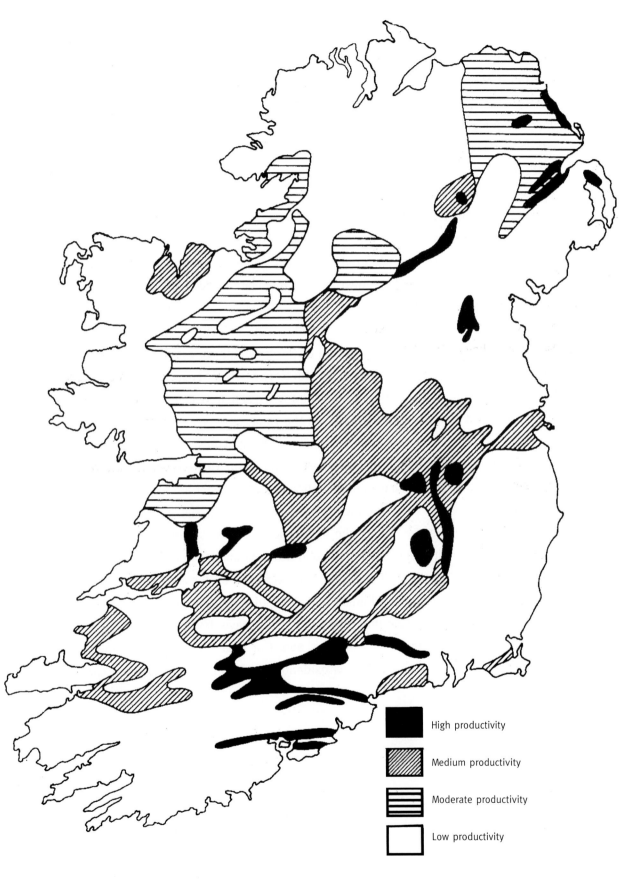

High productivity

Medium productivity

Moderate productivity

Low productivity

Rock Aquifers

Soil parent materials

Parent material is one of the five conventionally recognised factors of soil formation, the other four being climate, biota, topography and time. Parent material is the substance from which soils develop and is mainly of mineral (rock) origin, though in this country about 15% of our soils are developed in peaty and organic deposits. Our soils are developing in crushed and weathered debris and sediments, rather than from unbroken rock. The exceptions are steep slopes and some high mountain plateaux and crests. In its many waxings and wanings the ice quarried, abraded, etched, scoured, ground and comminuted the bedrock over which it travelled and incorporated into its load both fresh rock debris and older soils and sediments. This material has been deposited unsorted or, if meltwaters were involved, the deposits are stratified and sorted. The term drift incorporates both; the unsorted material is generally referred to as "till" and the sorted and stratified material known as "glaciofluvial" or "fluvioglacial". Glaciomarine drift has a sea-bed origin.

This map is a rough generalisation of the geographical extent of the main materials from which our mineral soils have developed. There are parallels between the boundaries on this map and those of the solid-geology maps (page 26, plate 4). In other words, the local rock has "left its mark" on the character of local soils. It is common to hear expressions such as "the limestone soils of the midlands", "the sandstone soils of Munster", "the basaltic soils of the northeast", and so on. However we cannot carry this generalisation too far. The limestone-floored valleys of Munster are filled with sandstone and shale debris from the surrounding hills; siliceous material from west Mayo and Galway forms a broken veneer on the limestones to the east; limestone till has been carried many kilometres onto the granite and other mountains in Leinster, and mud and ooze from the bed of the Irish sea have been smeared on the land surface of eastern counties Down, Meath, Dublin, Kildare and Wexford. Even though Co. Wicklow has no limestone bedrock, a sizeable proportion of its soils have developed in lime-rich materials brought in by ice thousands of years ago. Our peat soils have developed where drainage has been insufficient to allow oxidation and biological activity to occur.

Culleton, E.B. and Gardiner, M.J., 1985. Soil Formation. Chapter 7 in: The Quaternary History of Ireland, edited by K.J. Edwards and W.P. Warren. Academic Press, London.

1 Limestone drift
2 Limestone bedrock, thin drift
3 Sandstone till & bedrock
4 Lower Paleozoic shale/slate
   till; sandstone in places
5 Schist/gneiss/quartzite till &
   bedrock
6 Acid igneous/quartzite till &
   bedrock
7 Basalt till & bedrock
8 Glaciomarine drift
9 Upper Carboniferous shale

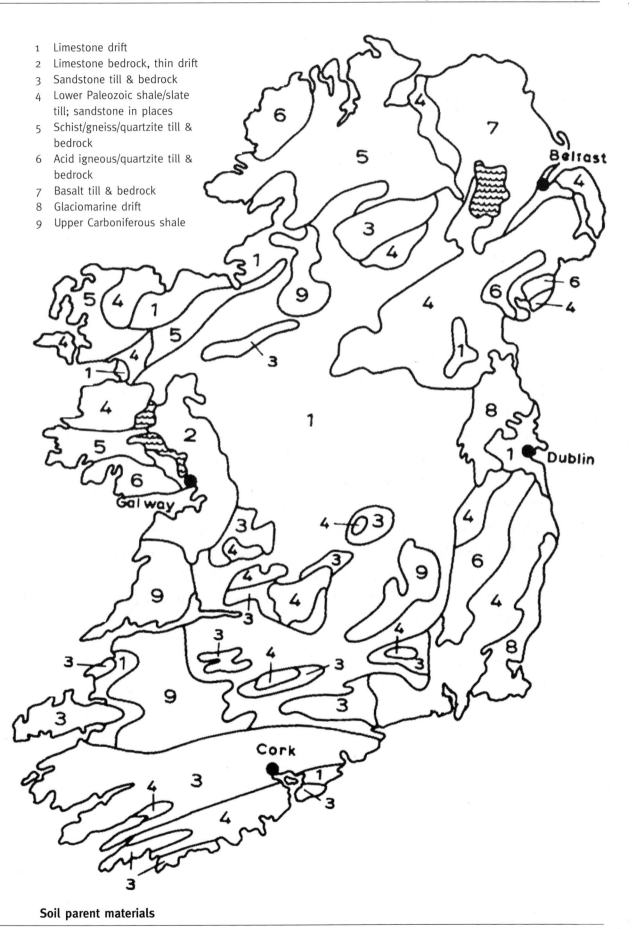

Soil parent materials

Pedogenic processes

Pedogenic processes are mechanisms leading to the formation of soils and their horizons. They are controlled chiefly by climatic conditions and parent material. Since Ireland is located in the humid temperate mid latitudes, with precipitation exceeding evapotranspiration, our soils reflect conditions of moderate temperature and some excess water. The processes listed with this map (podzolisation, illuviation, gleying, peat accumulation) are compound processes, made up of physical, chemical and biological reactions. The process shown for any location is the dominant one and many other processes occur simultaneously.

The term podzolisation includes acidification, organic-matter accumulation at the surface, and leaching downward of mobile iron, aluminium and clay. It may include induration and iron-pan formation. It is best expressed where the parent materials are silica-rich and coarse-textured and the vegetation type was acid-forming.

Gleying processes are caused by wetness due to a high water table or to low hydraulic conductivity of the soil or subsoil: lack of biological activity, organic matter accumulation, structural collapse and limited rooting are examples. Gleying is a widespread condition on the fine-textured shales, basalts and throughout the drumlin landscapes.

Clay illuviation is the downward movement of layer-silicate clays and involves entrainment, deflocculation, transport and re-flocculation. It is most widespread where the parent material is base rich, conditions are free-draining, and where the dominant vegetation has been broadleaved deciduous woodland.

Peat development involves reduced air penetration, poor oxidation, compaction and the synthesis of new organic chemical compounds.

"Minimal development" reflects the situations where conditions are not conducive to soil or soil horizon formation. A variety of reasons may be responsible: highly calcareous rock; highly unreactive parent material; steep slopes; recent deposits and others. Some soils show little profile development since processes that form horizons are retarded by opposing trends, such as mixing by plants and animals or erosion.

Culleton, E.B. and Gardiner, M.J., 1985. Soil Formation. Chapter 7 in: The Quaternary History of Ireland, edited by K.J. Edwards and W.P. Warren. Academic Press, London.

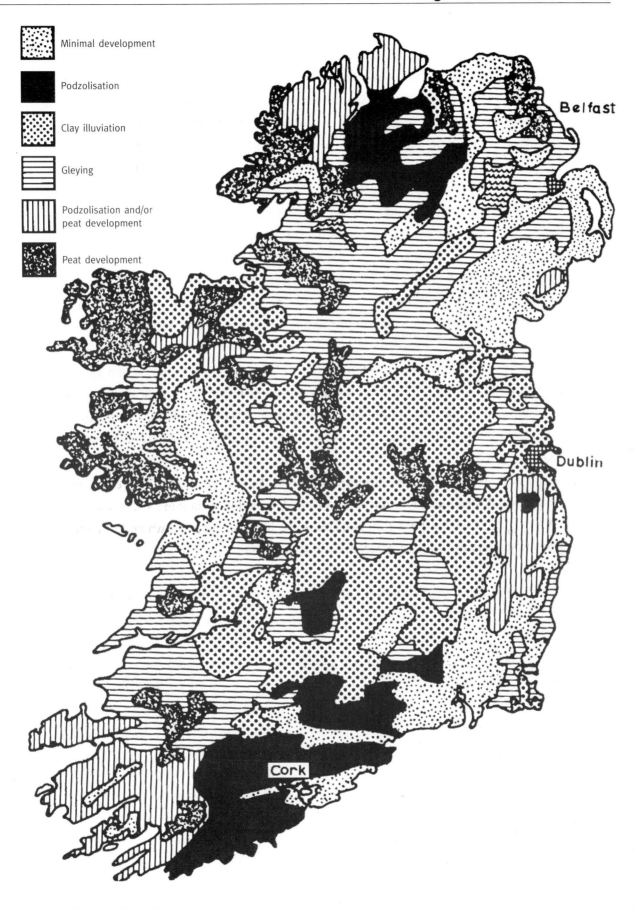

Minimal development

Podzolisation

Clay illuviation

Gleying

Podzolisation and/or
peat development

Peat development

Belfast

Dublin

Cork

Dominant pedogenic processes

Wealth in Ireland has long been centred on the soil resource and from time immemorial its reputation for agricultural productivity has been acclaimed. However only in recent years has any attempt been made to accurately assess the nature and extent of this resource. Despite the large volume of data compiled during the Townland Valuation of the 1830–1850 period by Griffith and his team of valuators, the objective study of the geographical distribution of our soils had to wait until this century. Research in the 1940's had its fruition when the Agricultural Institute established a National Soil Survey in the late 1950's. Slow but steady progress was made in mapping individual counties during the 1960's and 1970's and the first Ireland-wide soil map was published in 1969, followed by an up-dated edition in 1980. A five-year project to map the soils of the Northern Ireland counties has recently been completed.

This is a simplified, generalised and reduced depiction of a Soil Associations map, with modifications of the legend to make it compatible with the FAO soil map of Europe. While the terms podzol (a leached soil with strongly-developed horizons) and gleysol (a waterlogged, grey soil) are fairly well known, it can be noted that luvisol is equivalent to grey-brown podzolic (soil with a clay-enriched subsoil), cambisol to brown earth (soil with little horizon development) and histosol to organic (peat) soil. This map, and the more detailed county maps, help us to understand the pattern of land use, the areas of environmental or geographic disadvantage and to compare our agricultural resources with those of our neighbours with whom we compete for markets, quotas and price supports.

Plate 6 is a coloured version of this map.

Diamond, S. (private communication, 1995). Teagasc, Johnstown Castle, Wexford.
Gardiner, M.J. and Radford, T., 1980. *Soil Associations of Ireland and Their Land Use Potential. Soil Survey Bulletin No. 36*, An Foras Talúntais, Dublin.

1.   Podzol

2.   Podzol—leptic

3.   Luvisol

4.   Cambisol

5.   Gleysol

6.   Cambisol—eutric

7.   Rendzina & lithosol

8.   Histosol—raised

9.   Histosol—blanket

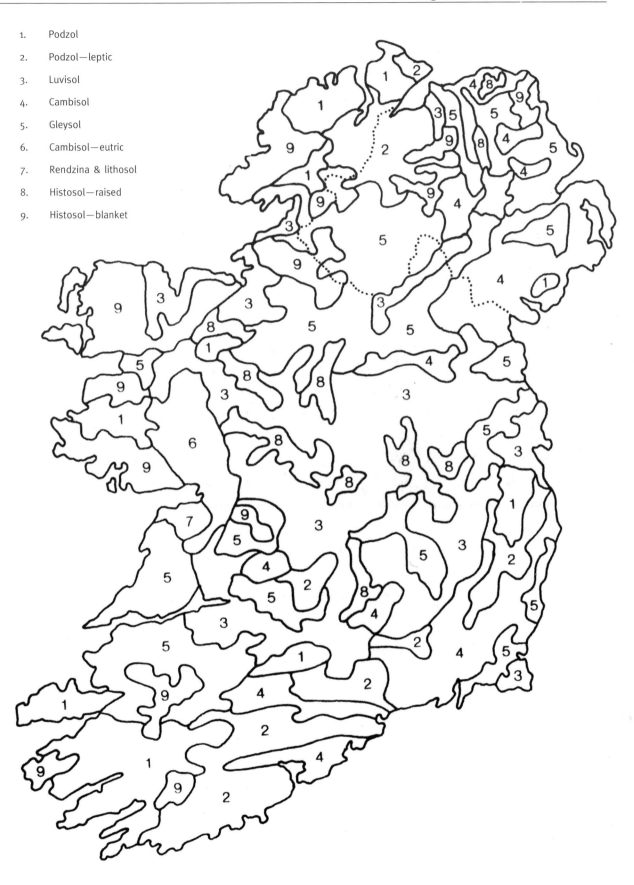

Soil great groups, based on the Soil Map of Ireland, 1980

Blanket bog

Peat is an accumulation of dead organisms usually of plant origin and occurs wherever conditions prevent decomposing organisms from returning all the carbon to the atmosphere as carbon dioxide gas. These conditions include standing water (as in still lakes) excess soil water (where precipitation greatly exceeds drainage and evapo-transpiration) and extreme acidity (caused by acid geology or acid-generating plants). In Ireland, these conditions are assisted by low temperatures on hills and in winter.

Peatland development in Ireland varies according to a combination of predisposing conditions, and gives rise to several distinct peat types.

These four maps depict the occurrence of blanket bog in Ireland. The term 'blanket' is used interchangeably with 'climatic' and occasionally with 'hill and mountain' in this context. Hence one can visualise this kind of peat (1) clothing the rocks and soils of the country as a blanket; (2) depending on the climate of the locality for its existence or (3) confined to, and best-developed on, the more elevated parts of the country.

The word "bog" signifies a unit of land and is used interchangeably with other terms such as moor, moss, mire, quagmire, swamp or peatland.

The blanket bog sub-type "Atlantic" has a particular association of bog plants which proliferate at low altitude (usually < 150 m in western Ireland). The main distinguishing plant is the black bog rush (*Schoenus nigricans* L.). Montane refers to 'mountain' and includes peat at altitudes higher than approximately 150 m, where *S. nigricans* is absent. The term 'man modified' emphasises that man has been intruding on the bog landscapes of Ireland for many centuries, mainly by hand cutting for fuel, and land reclamation around the bog edges.

Hammond, R.F., 1981. The Peatlands of Ireland. Soil Survey Bulletin No. 35, An Foras Talúntais, Dublin.

Distribution of blanket bog types: (a) Atlantic sub-type; (b) montane sub-type; (c) man-modified Atlantic sub-type; (d) man-modified montane sub-type

Raised bog and fen peats

In contrast with the blanket peats which were dependent on the climate for their existence, the midland peats (raised bogs and fens) developed in open bodies of water. Eventually, the fens became elevated by growth of sphagnum mosses, by virtue of the moss being able to survive on the meagre nutrition supplied in precipitation. The industrial peats are those large expanses which are exploited mechanically for fuel, and are mostly raised bogs. The term man-modified refers to reclamation, drainage, cutting, burning and other operations that have drastically changed the nature of these peatlands.

Fen peat is a relatively shallow peat which may form a natural landscape unit or may be a layer/deposit covered by meters of other kinds of peat especially raised domes. It is formed from dead vegetation which grew in a mineral-rich environment, and hence left this peat type relatively rich in nutrients (eg. calcium, magnesium and potassium). These are the most versatile of peats, suitable for many purposes when drained. With the exception of the internationally important Pollardstown Fen in Co. Kildare, there are no large areas of unmodified fen peat in this country. (The Fenlands of E. England are a good example of the agricultural exploitation of this resource). A number of projects aimed at restoring some of our least altered raised bogs to a wetter state are in progress.

Hammond, R.F., 1981. The Peatlands of Ireland. Soil Survey Bulletin No. 35, An Foras Talúntais, Dublin.

(a)

(b)

(c)

(d)

Distribution of raised bogs and fen peats: (a) industrial peat areas; (b) raised bog—man modified; (c) fen peat—man modified; (d) raised bog—unmodified

Soils of Co. Laois

This is a map of the soil series in the northeast part of Co. Laois. It is a section of the soil map of the whole county, published with Soil Survey Bulletin No. 41 in 1987 by Teagasc (formerly An Foras Talúntais). It shows the distribution of the various series, complexes and phases and the legend records the placement of these mapping units in the various great groups (grey brown podzolic, brown earth, gley, peat). Definitions of these soil types are given in the Soil Survey Bulletins. Each series is composed mainly (but not exclusively) of one kind of soil, as evidenced by its morphological, physical and chemical properties. Each is given a name—usually that of the location where it was first mapped or where its greatest extent was found. Some of the names used in Co. Laois are imported from other counties since similar soils have been mapped previously in other counties. Examples are Fontstown from Co. Kildare, Patrickswell from Co Limerick, Banagher from Co. Offaly. Where a complicated mosaic of contrasting soils occurs it is usual to map the area as a soil complex and simply list its components in the accompanying text. Complexes are common along river valleys, in outwash plains and in hilly regions. Phases of series are identified where the soils of an area differ from the "local" or "dominant" soil in some single characteristic such as slope, depth or stoniness. Two phases were mapped in this part of Co. Laois—Stradbally Rocky Phase and Mylerstown Imperfectly-drained Phase.

The placement of a soil into categories (phases, series, great groups) enables us to organise our knowledge about soils, to interpret their characteristics and likely behaviour for a variety of land uses and to extend the findings of research from the research location to a relatively large geographical area. An interpretative map of this part of Co. Laois is presented later. Similar soil type and interpretative maps are now available for about half of our counties.

A colour version of this map is presented in plate 7.

S. Diamond (private communication, 1995). Teagasc, Johnstown Castle, Co. Wexford.

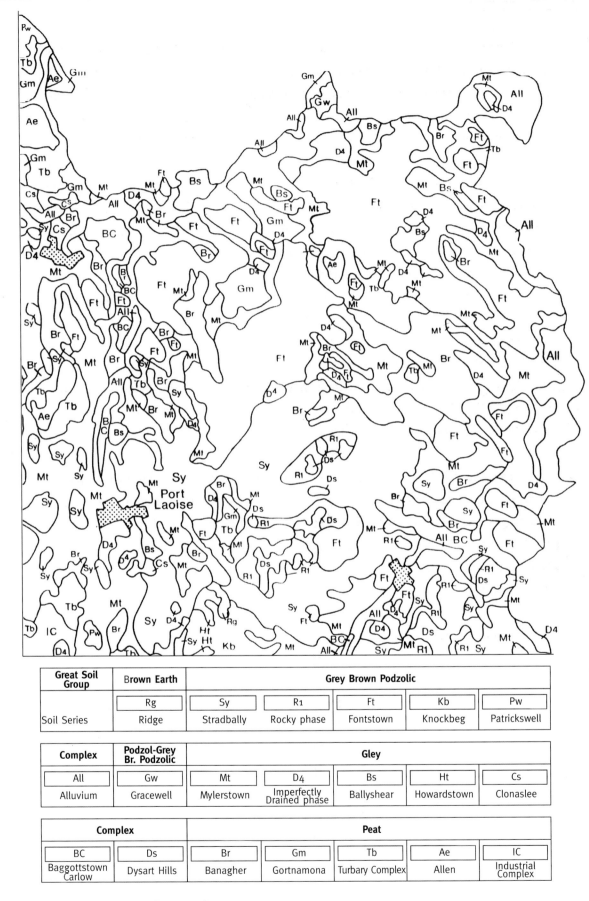

Great Soil Group	Brown Earth	Grey Brown Podzolic				
	Rg	Sy	R1	Ft	Kb	Pw
Soil Series	Ridge	Stradbally	Rocky phase	Fontstown	Knockbeg	Patrickswell

Complex	Podzol-Grey Br. Podzolic	Gley				
	All	Gw	Mt	D4	Bs	Ht	Cs
	Alluvium	Gracewell	Mylerstown	Imperfectly Drained phase	Ballyshear	Howardstown	Clonaslee

Complex		Peat				
BC	Ds	Br	Gm	Tb	Ae	IC
Baggottstown Carlow	Dysart Hills	Banagher	Gortnamona	Turbary Complex	Allen	Industrial Complex

Soil series of part of Co. Laois

Detailed soil map

An Foras Talúntais (now Teagasc) operated an Economic Test Farm near Herbertstown, Co. Limerick in the 1960's–'70's. In order that the data collected there be applicable to as wide/extensive an area as possible, a detailed map of the soils of the 28 ha (70 acre) farm was made. It was then possible to relate these soils to those of Co. Limerick in general.

The legend records the Soil series (Elton, Howardstown, Rootiagh), the drainage status (well to poor) and the parent materials (predominantly limestone and basalt drift). The published report discusses the soils and environmental conditions (altitude, slope, climate) while the map shows the distribution and extent of the various soils. The authors point out that the temperature values used (from the nearest synoptic station at Shannon Airport, situated in an estuary 90 m (300 feet) lower than the farm) were not strictly applicable to the Herbertstown area.

Nevertheless the findings on this test farm have had implications for extensive areas in Co. Limerick (Elton series, about 7,200 ha (180,000 acres), Herbertstown series, 46,400 ha (116,000 acres) and Rootiagh, 320 ha (800 acres)) and to other places with similar soils and environmental conditions elsewhere.

Detailed soil maps (scale 1:1000; 1:2500) are usually commmissioned for farms attached to agricultural research and teaching institutions, as well as for areas of scientific or environmental importance such as National Parks.

Finch, T.F., 1964. Economic Test Farm Herbertstown, Co. Limerick. Soil Survey Bulletin No. 7, An Foras Talúntais, Dublin.

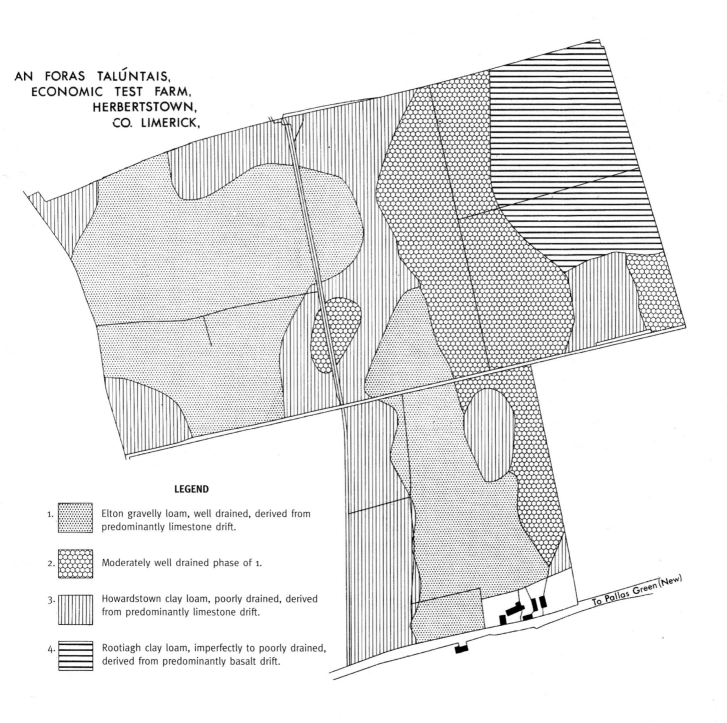

AN FORAS TALÚNTAIS,
ECONOMIC TEST FARM,
HERBERTSTOWN,
CO. LIMERICK,

To Pallas Green (New)

LEGEND

1. Elton gravelly loam, well drained, derived from predominantly limestone drift.

2. Moderately well drained phase of 1.

3. Howardstown clay loam, poorly drained, derived from predominantly limestone drift.

4. Rootiagh clay loam, imperfectly to poorly drained, derived from predominantly basalt drift.

Detailed soil map of Herbertstown Economic Test Farm, Co. Limerick

Land drainage problems

Over 60% of Irish land (nearer 75% in Northern Ireland) has significant wetness characteristics and in some cases is waterlogged and swampy. It is dominated by hydrophilic vegetation (rushes, meadowsweet, purple moor grass, sedges, reeds, mosses and many others) unless drained. Using the agricultural advisory service, granting agencies and other government personnel dealing with farmers, it was possible to prepare a map, at 9 inches to 1 mile, of the causes of land wetness and the regions dominated by each cause. This is a much reduced version of the original, and the legend below is presented in its entirety.

Drainage problem	No.	Description
Water table	1	The level of the free-water surface (phreatic surface) is so high that drains must be installed to lower it.
Seepage outburst and spring	2	Outburst of underground water (artesian) over a wide area near the bottom of a slope (seepage outburst) or at a particular point (spring).
Cemented layer	3	A layer of bonded subsoil resulting in an impervious layer at a relatively shallow depth.
Iron pan	4	A thin high-iron layer forming an impervious pan.
Impervious subsoil	5	The subsoil has such low permeability that the rate of water flow through it is restricted considerably.
Impervious topsoil	6	The topsoil is so imperious that it inhibits the rate of water flow through the surface. This can sometimes occur over a permeable subsoil.
Impervious layer	7	A soil layer which is not cemented but which prevents the passage of water because of its low permeability.
Natural hollows	8	Large depressions that require deep cuts to provide drainage.
Flooding	9	Land that is often covered by water due to its low-level position beside river, stream or sea.
Not classified	10	Land above 600 feet (183m) O.D.

It is to be emphasised that the map indicates the drainage problem most frequently found in the regions shown. Large areas unaffected by drainage problems occur in all regions.

Galvin, L.F., 1971. Land Drainage Survey III Maps of Ireland showing the general distribution of drainage problems and of drainage schemes. Irish Journal of Agricultural Research 10: 213–221.

1 High water table
2 Seepage outburst and spring
3 Cemented layer
4 Iron pan
5 Impervious subsoil
6 Impervious topsoil
7 Impervious layer
8 Natural hollows
9 Flooding
10 Land above 600 feet (183m)

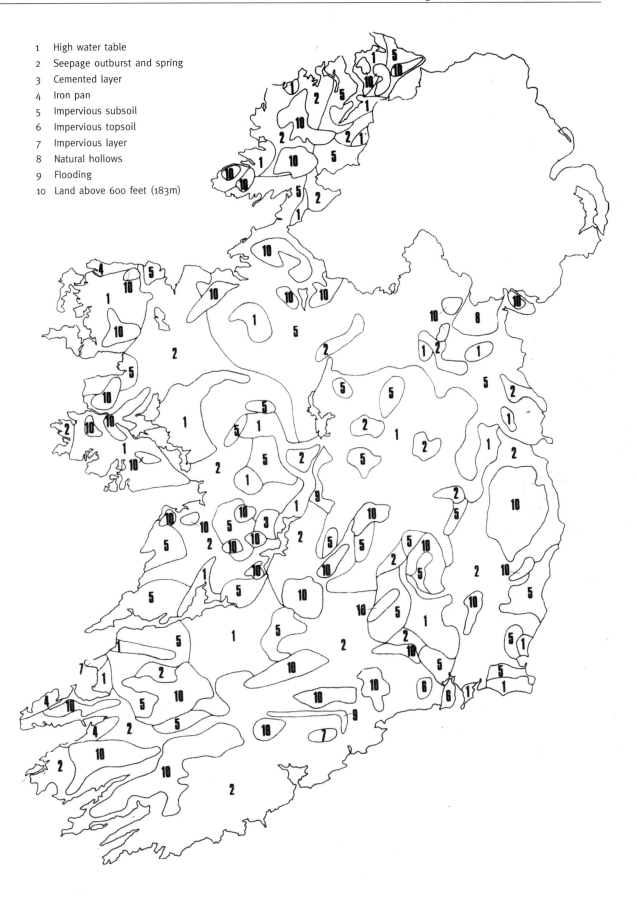

Land drainage problems

Arterial and field drainage

In common with much of Europe, Ireland has a long history of land drainage—a term which generally includes two types of drainage: arterial and field. Arterial drainage involves the artificial widening, deepening and straightening of main rivers and their tributaries in order to more effectively remove water from their catchments. Field drainage is an on-farm operation which involves the making (and remaking) of series of open and closed drains and ditches to remove surplus water from fields. From an agricultural point of view both types are interdependent and complimentary—the benefit of one being contingent on progress on the other.

Arterial drainage in Ireland is the responsibility of the State, the beginnings of which can be traced through the Office of Public Works and the Board of Works to famine times when about 40,000 persons were involved in this activity. Expenditure on arterial drainage has expanded and contracted with government policy, economic prosperity and perceived flood hazard or damage. It has generally been very successful in providing an outlet for field drains and in reducing the likelihood of floods to cropland in the critical spring to autumn period. However there are many undesirable side-effects which have questioned the overall benefits:

- interference with private and public water supplies;
- damage to vegetation, fish stocks, wildlife and the aesthetic character of river valleys;
- reduction of the capacity of rivers and worsening of flooding in some places.

Field drainage is the responsibility of individual land owners and has been state aided with grants since the 1930s. Its technology has changed with advances in excavation, pipe manufacture and knowledge of soil properties. It has enabled thousands of hectares to be used for a wider variety of crops, extended growing and grazing seasons, reduced the incidence of many diseases and improved farm incomes.

These maps show the percentage of farmland, at county scale, which has undergone arterial and field drainage. Over 20% of Irish agricultural land (about 3 million acres = 1.2 million hectares) has had field drainage. This compares with about 54% in Denmark, 61% in the UK, 65% in the Netherlands, 74% in Hungary and 91% (of agricultural land) in Finland

Bruton, R. and Convery, F.J., 1982. Land drainage policy in Ireland. Policy Research Series 4, Economic and Social Research Institute, Dublin.

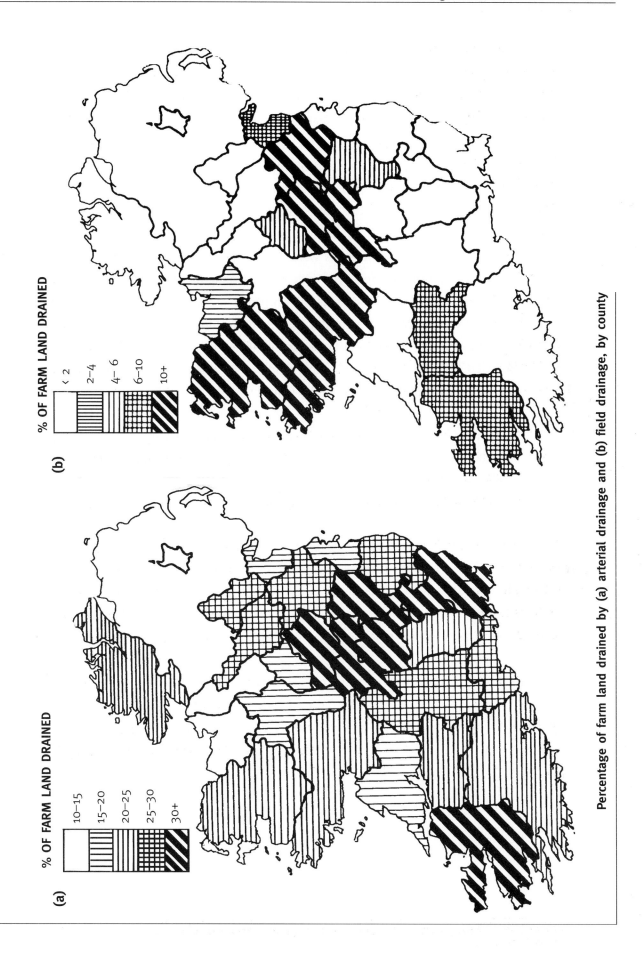

(b)

% OF FARM LAND DRAINED

< 2
2– 4
4– 6
6–10
10+

(a)

% OF FARM LAND DRAINED

10–15
15–20
20–25
25–30
30+

Percentage of farm land drained by (a) arterial drainage and (b) field drainage, by county

Arable cropping

Less than 10% of Irish agricultural land is used for arable crops. This map shows that most of that land is in east Leinster and parts of south Munster. Reference to other maps in this atlas will show that this part of the country has a number of advantages which lead to better opportunities for seedbed preparation and harvesting, as well as promoting higher yields. These advantages include lower annual rainfalls, fewer wet days, higher temperatures, less likelihood of frost, higher radiation receipts and more hours of bright sunshine. Within that area there are some exceptions due to soil limitations (such as wetness, slope, droughts, flooding) but since soils of similar characteristics are common in most Irish counties, the dictating factor is mostly climatological. In the past when oats and potatoes were more common, the geographical distribution of tillage was much different. Even within today's range of crops, not all of them will be equally spread through the areas shown. Good examples are sugar beet and early potatoes which do best on a coastal strip from Wexford to west Cork. Access to markets (such as Belfast, Dublin and Cork) also influence the general pattern—in particular, north Co. Dublin has a rate of arable cropping far higher than its rather heavy soils alone would suggest, even with its low rainfall.

Grassland or pastoral farming dominates the remainder of the agricultural land of the country. Much of it is used for dairying in Munster, drystock farming in midland and western counties, sheeprearing, especially in the more marginal lands, and for the bloodstock industry in select areas such as central Co. Kildare.

Gillmor, D. (editor), 1979. Irish Resources and Land Use. Institute of Public Administration, Dublin.

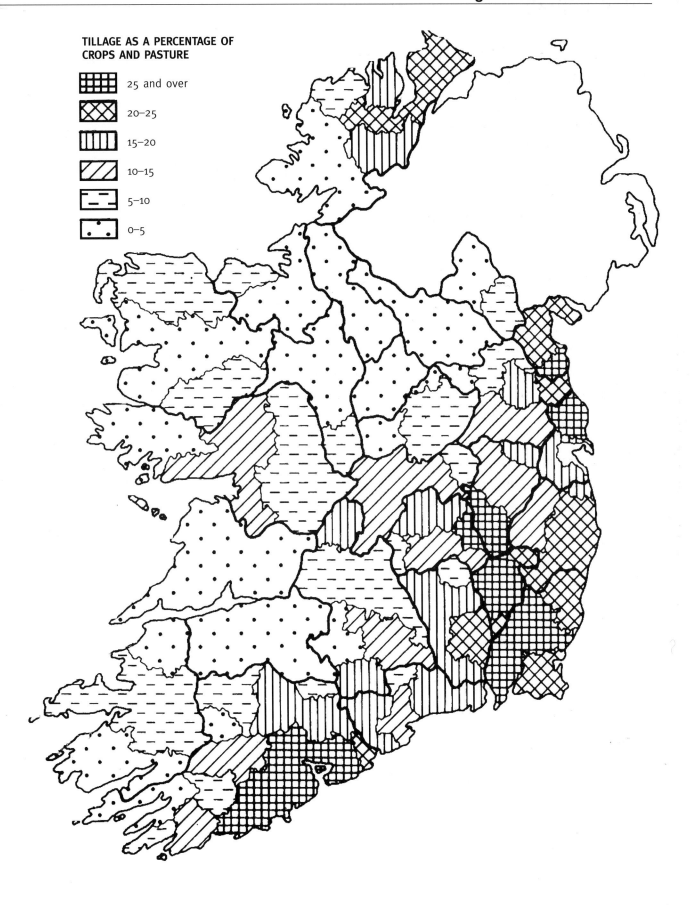

TILLAGE AS A PERCENTAGE OF
CROPS AND PASTURE

25 and over

20–25

15–20

10–15

5–10

0–5

Tillage as a percentage of crops and pasture, by rural area

Lowland grasslands

About 250 species of vascular plants are to be found in Irish grasslands. An individual grass field may have 15 to 45 species. Very intensively farmed grassland is typically species-poor and usually dominated by perennial ryegrass and white clover. Unimproved grassland can have up to 45 species. Some species like bentgrass, Yorkshire fog and common buttercup occur in virtually all grassland types. Others like cowslip and bog thistle are restricted to ecologically well-defined grassland types.

This map is based on a national grassland survey carried out between 1965 and 1975. The boundaries between grassland types are drawn with the aid of national soil mapping data, which correlate well with grassland types.

1. High and moderately-high quality pasture and meadow on deep, well-drained soils. They have a low species number and are usually dominated by perennial ryegrass.

2. Moderate quality pasture and meadow on well- to over-drained, shallow limestone soils. They have a high species number and include lime-loving species like cowslip and golden oatgrass.

3. Moderate- to poor-quality pasture and meadow on imperfectly- to poorly-drained soils. They have a high species number and are typically dominated by rush and sedge species.

4. Heathy grassland, bracken-dominated grazings, dry heather and furze heathlands on podzols, peaty podzols and drier shallow peats. They mainly occur on the lower slopes of hills and mountains in the east and south.

4a Burren grasslands on skeletal (shallow) soils over limestone. They are typically dominated by blue moor-grass and contain a large number of rare and attractive herbs like mountain avens, gentian and bloody cranesbill.

1/3 Complexes of Type 1 and Type 3.

The blank areas are mainly blanket bogs and raised bogs which have their own unique vegetation.

O'Sullivan, A.M., 1982. *The lowland grasslands of Ireland*, in: *Studies on Irish Vegetation*, edited by J. White. Royal Dublin Society, Dublin.

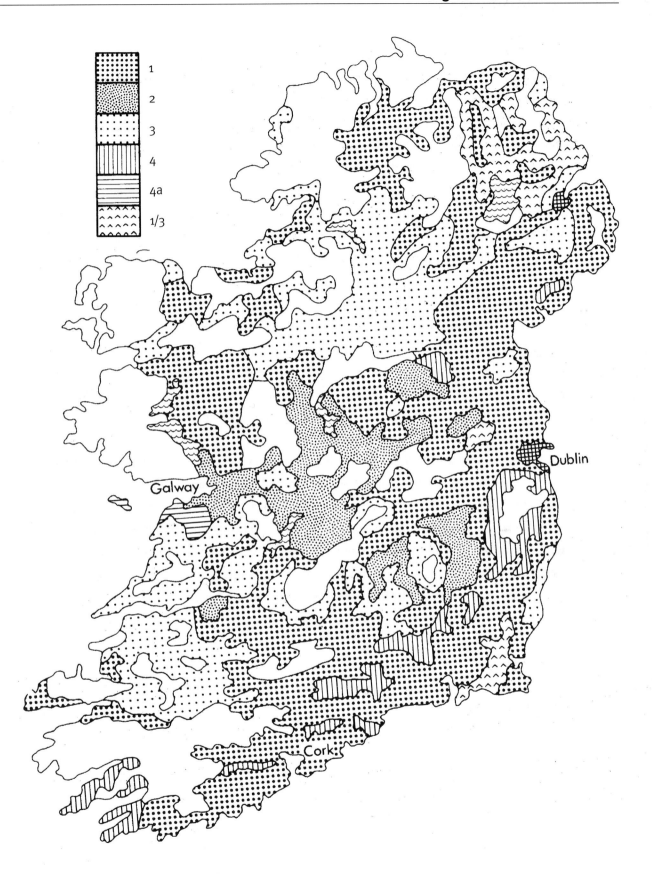

Main lowland grassland types (legend explained opposite)

Forests

These maps give an impression of the extent of forests in Ireland in the sixteenth and late twentieth centuries. Neither is comprehensive, but they do reflect the major factors controlling the location of forests. Map (a) is a reconstruction from a large variety of historical and some palynological sources of the likely extent and location of forest in the sixteenth century. There was a large extent of forest, although the majority of the land had already been cleared leaving forest areas in lowland situations, especially river valleys. An explanation of this pattern may be that the mouldboard plough had not yet been introduced, and only the coulter plough and spade were available for cultivation. This plough was not suited to heavy soils, and it is believed that tillage at this time was mostly on sloping land at moderate elevations where the soils were lighter.

Following four centuries of major impacts to forests, about 1% of the land remained under tree cover at the start of the twentieth century. Most of this was within estate walls, or was scrub-quality woodland in inaccessible places. State forestry properties about 1980 are shown in map (b). This excludes the remaining estate woods and the scraps of native woodland just mentioned. The areas shown also include some small unplanted areas, most of which are uneconomic to plant due to poor fertility.

The forestry areas are scattered throughout the island, but their exact locations are related strongly to soils. About half the forest plantation area in the 1980s was on peatlands, and much of the rest was on mineral soils, possessing low fertility or impeded drainage. Forestry is virtually absent in some intensive farming areas such as the Golden Vale area. Since this map was produced, a large increase has occurred in the extent of private afforestation of land by farmers and investors. The expansion has partly occurred on peatland areas but in concentrated on wet mineral soils.

McCracken, E., 1971. *The Irish Woods Since Tudor Times. David & Charles, Newton Abbot.*
Forest Service, Dublin.

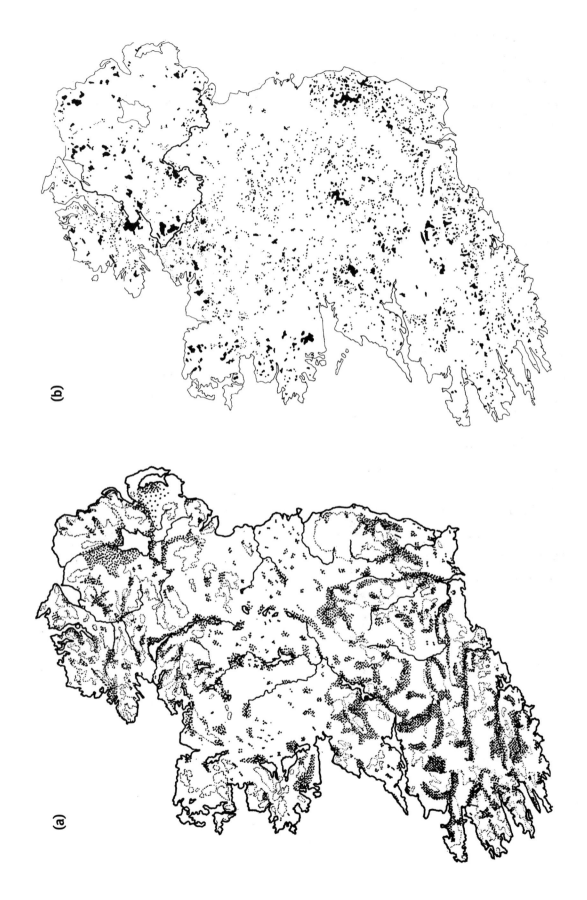

Forests: (a) the likely extent of forest about 1600; (b) state forest land, 1980

The fish-farming industry

While dairy farmers may be concerned about earliness of grass growth, cereal farmers about harvest weather and horticulturists about unseasonal frosts, fish farmers worry about shelter. One of the reasons why fish farming developed in Ireland in the last 25 years was the availability of an excellent physical environment along our western coast. A heavily indented coastline has provided sheltered sites in pollution-free water. One of the few natural hazards is the chance of gales and storms from which even the most sheltered bay or fjord cannot hide. The rafts, cages, floats and other structures involve a considerable investment and need to be sensibly located in the first instance.

Fish farming started off with fresh water trout farms in the clear upper stretches of rivers, but in the late 1970's changed to salmon farming based on smolt from the ESB hatcheries. Salmon farming is concentrated on the north and west coasts, while many of the hatcheries are found in onshore sites nearby, as well as in a cluster in Co. Wicklow. Sea trout is operated as a sector of the salmon farming and is generally overshadowed by the freshwater sector. Most of the latter's installations are located in the southeast (map (a)).

Some of the concerns of the fresh water farms centre around extremes of water supply—too little may reduce tank levels and allow pollution to concentrate downstream; too much rain may cause flooding and damage to property.

The two main kinds of shell fish farmed here are mussels and oysters. The mussel farms are concentrated in the southwest, especially Bantry and Kenmare Bays (map (b)). Intensive fish farming involves cultivating mussels on ropes or poles suspended from rafts or floats, while extensive farming involves dredging seed mussels and relaying them in prepared sea-bottom beds in sheltered locations. One of the climatically related diseases to hit the enterprise is the occasional occurrence of phytoplankton bloom known as "red tide". The main concentrations of oyster farms are in Carlingford Lough, Clew Bay and Galway Bay.

Colour wall charts showing the distribution of other types of fish farming have been published by Bord Iascaigh Mhara. These types include abalone, clams, scallops and sea urchins.

Breathnach, P., 1992. The development of the fish farming industry. Irish Geography 25 (2): 182–187.

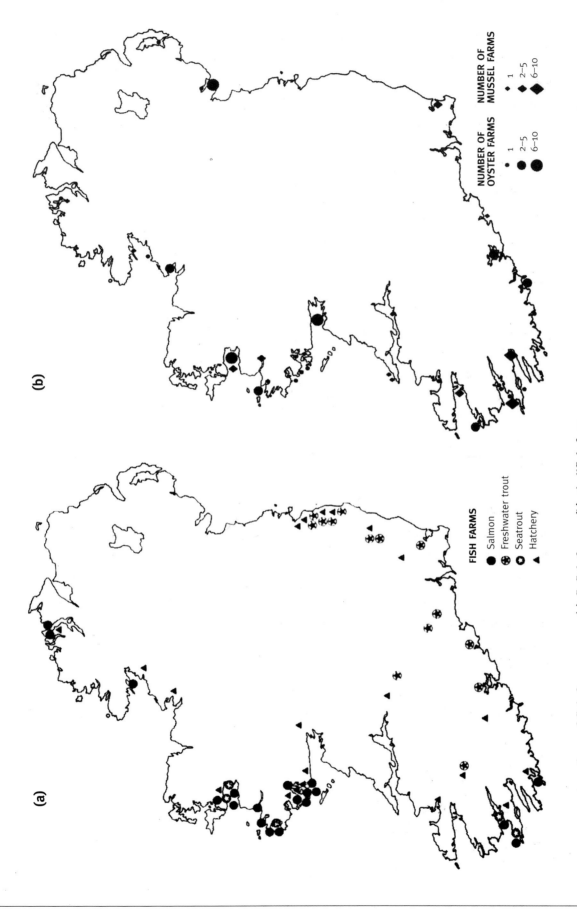

(b)

(a)

FISH FARMS
● Salmon
✷ Freshwater trout
✪ Seatrout
◀ Hatchery

NUMBER OF
OYSTER FARMS
• 1
● 2–5
● 6–10

NUMBER OF
MUSSEL FARMS
♦ 1
♦ 2–5
♦ 6–10

Locations of fish farms, 1990: (a) finfish farms; (b) shellfish farms

The coast

The coastline of Ireland exhibits a variety of rocks and scenery scarcely matched anywhere else. The rocks range in age from the oldest Precambrian to the most recent, and in structure from vertical, bevelled and stepped cliffs to slumped blocks; in between are ice-eroded troughs, low drift cliffs, sand dunes, drowned river valleys and elevated beach platforms.

The sandstone structures of Munster form the bays and peninsulas of Cork and Kerry. Many features of the north and west result from fault lines (Clew Bay, Lough Swilly, Lough Foyle, Belfast Lough); in between, ice has honed the finer details such as corries on Achill and the north side of Donegal Bay. Precipitous cliffs develop where natural planes of weakness in rocks are vertical, as has happened in vertically-oriented volcanics (Wexford) and more widely in limestones which have planes of weakness at right angles to the horizontal bedding planes (Clare, Aran, north Mayo). Resistant sandstones, granites and gneisses give rugged coastlines (Cork, Kerry, Donegal, Down). The softer tills form low cliffs when under-cut by sea waves (Mayo, Wexford, Meath, Dublin, Wicklow) and the produce is moved along to form beaches, bars and dunes. Many of these are well-known resorts — Brittas Bay, Dollymount, Dundrum Bay, Achill, Ballybunion, Tramore and Youghal. Some coasts are protected by embankments and dikes, most widely in Wexford Harbour, the Nore and Shannon estuaries and in Loughs Swilly and Foyle/Roe. Erosion of rock cliffs may occur at less than 1 m in 1000 years, but exceeds 1 m per year in some soft till cliffs along the east coast, with an estimated loss of 130–160 hectares of land annually, worth about a million pounds. The widespread occurrence of submerged or partially submerged peat and stumps of forest trees attest to former sea levels lower than they are now.

Agricultural enterprises on exposed coasts are subjected to wind damage (defoliation, abrasion, breakage and uprooting, erosion and sand drifting), salt spray, excessive leaching and in low-lying areas to salt-water intrusion. Some human activities have unintentionally accelerated erosion, including building of jetties, seawalls and harbours, dredging and aggregate extraction. Leisure activities may also disturb fragile dune systems.

Stephens, N., 1970. The Coastline of Ireland. Chapter 8 in: Irish Geographical Studies, edited by N. Stephens and R.E. Glassock, The Queen's University, Belfast.

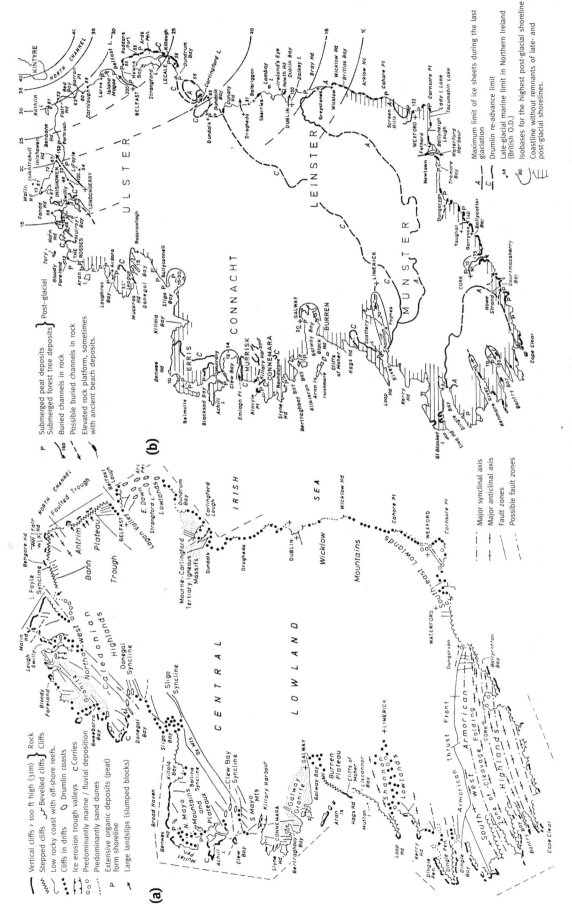

The coastline of Ireland: (a) structural elements and morphological features; (b) some Pleistocene and Holocene features

Plate 1. Corine Land Cover Map Composite

The CORINE (Co-ordination of Information on the Environment) Information System comprises a series of databases on the environment of use in the orientation, application and assessment of several European policies, but primarily environmental protection. This information includes important biotopes, atmospheric emissions, land cover, coastal erosion, soil erosion and water erosion.

The Land Cover database provides comprehensive data on biophysical land occupation that is consistent and comparable across Europe. The land cover inventory at a scale of 1:100,000 is based on computer assisted photo-interpretation of satellite images into 44 hierarchical categories, with the simultaneous consultation of ancillary data.

The CORINE Land Cover (Ireland) Project was carried out as a cooperative cross-border initiative jointly co-ordinated by the Ordnance Survey of Northern Ireland and the Ordnance Survey of Ireland.

This plate is a composite of CORINE map sheets C7 (Dublin) and C8 (Cork) which were published at 1:500,000 scale, reduced to approximately 1:2,500,000. Of the 44 hierarchical categories recognised across Europe, 38 were represented in Ireland. The most extensive category is "Pasture", and there are significant areas of "Peat bogs". Much of the "Agricultural areas" of Northern Ireland are placed in "Complex cultivation patterns", while in the Republic, most are placed in the "Non-irrigated arable" category. Compared with other maps, the area designated "Intertidal flats" is also notable.

European Environment Agency, Kogens Nytorv 6, DK-1050 Copenhagen.

Corine land cover map composite

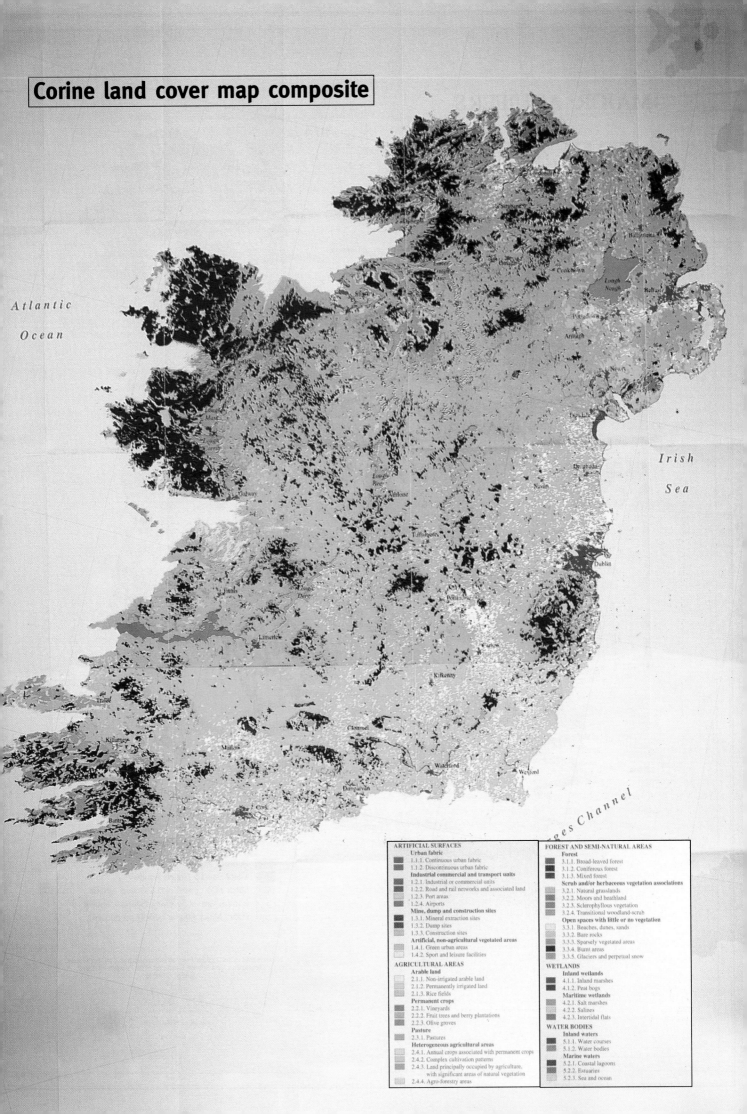

Atlantic

Ocean

Irish

Sea

...ges Channel

ARTIFICIAL SURFACES
Urban fabric
1.1.1. Continuous urban fabric
1.1.2. Discontinuous urban fabric
Industrial commercial and transport units
1.2.1. Industrial or commercial units
1.2.2. Road and rail networks and associated land
1.2.3. Port areas
1.2.4. Airports
Mine, dump and construction sites
1.3.1. Mineral extraction sites
1.3.2. Dump sites
1.3.3. Construction sites
Artificial, non-agricultural vegetated areas
1.4.1. Green urban areas
1.4.2. Sport and leisure facilities

AGRICULTURAL AREAS
Arable land
2.1.1. Non-irrigated arable land
2.1.2. Permanently irrigated land
2.1.3. Rice fields
Permanent crops
2.2.1. Vineyards
2.2.2. Fruit trees and berry plantations
2.2.3. Olive groves
Pasture
2.3.1. Pastures
Heterogeneous agricultural areas
2.4.1. Annual crops associated with permanent crops
2.4.2. Complex cultivation patterns
2.4.3. Land principally occupied by agriculture,
  with significant areas of natural vegetation
2.4.4. Agro-forestry areas

FOREST AND SEMI-NATURAL AREAS
Forest
3.1.1. Broad-leaved forest
3.1.2. Coniferous forest
3.1.3. Mixed forest
Scrub and/or herbaceous vegetation associations
3.2.1. Natural grasslands
3.2.2. Moors and heathland
3.2.3. Sclerophyllous vegetation
3.2.4. Transitional woodland-scrub
Open spaces with little or no vegetation
3.3.1. Beaches, dunes, sands
3.3.2. Bare rocks
3.3.3. Sparsely vegetated areas
3.3.4. Burnt areas
3.3.5. Glaciers and perpetual snow

WETLANDS
Inland wetlands
4.1.1. Inland marshes
4.1.2. Peat bogs
Maritime wetlands
4.2.1. Salt marshes
4.2.2. Salines
4.2.3. Intertidal flats

WATER BODIES
Inland waters
5.1.1. Water courses
5.1.2. Water bodies
Marine waters
5.2.1. Coastal lagoons
5.2.2. Estuaries
5.2.3. Sea and ocean

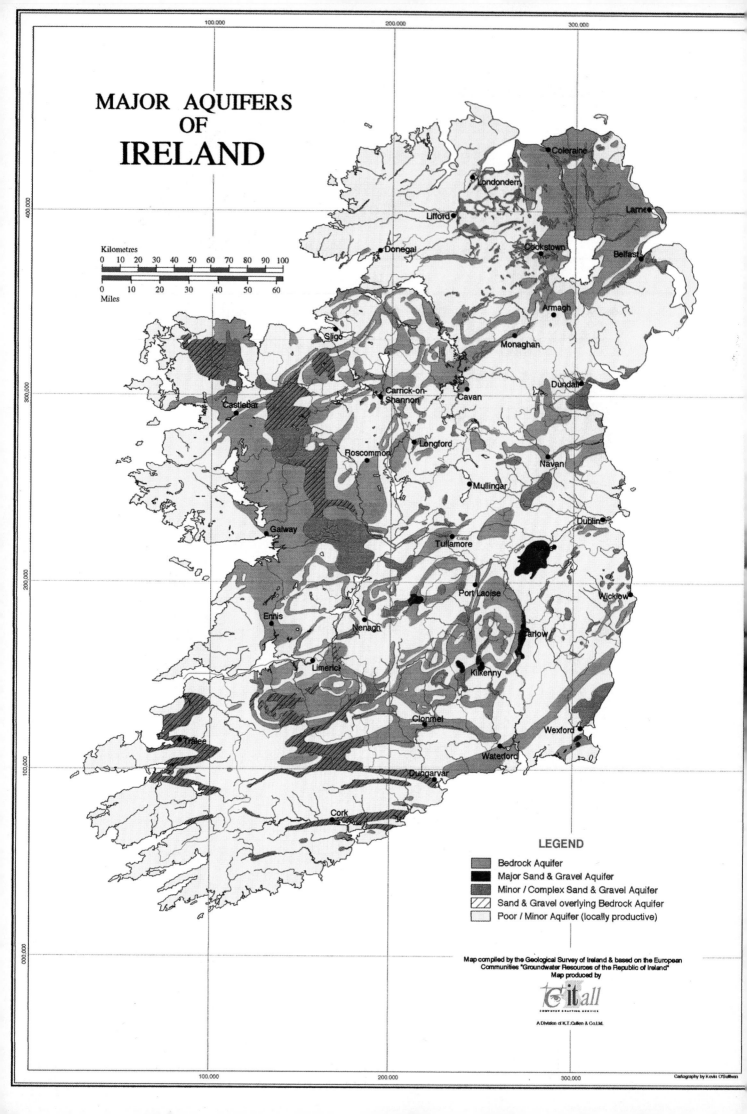

MAJOR AQUIFERS
OF
IRELAND

Kilometres
0 10 20 30 40 50 60 70 80 90 100

0 10 20 30 40 50 60
Miles

Coleraine
Londonderry
Lifford
Larne
Donegal
Cookstown
Belfast
Armagh
Sligo
Monaghan
Dundalk
Carrick-on-Shannon
Cavan
Castlebar
Longford
Navan
Roscommon
Mullingar
Dublin
Galway
Tullamore
Port Laoise
Wicklow
Ennis
Nenagh
Carlow
Limerick
Kilkenny
Clonmel
Wexford
Tralee
Waterford
Dungarvan
Cork

LEGEND

Bedrock Aquifer
Major Sand & Gravel Aquifer
Minor / Complex Sand & Gravel Aquifer
Sand & Gravel overlying Bedrock Aquifer
Poor / Minor Aquifer (locally productive)

Map compiled by the Geological Survey of Ireland & based on the European
Communities "Groundwater Resources of the Republic of Ireland"
Map produced by

Citall
COMPUTER DRAFTING SERVICE

A Division of K.T.Cullen & Co.Ltd.

Cartography by Kevin O'Sullivan

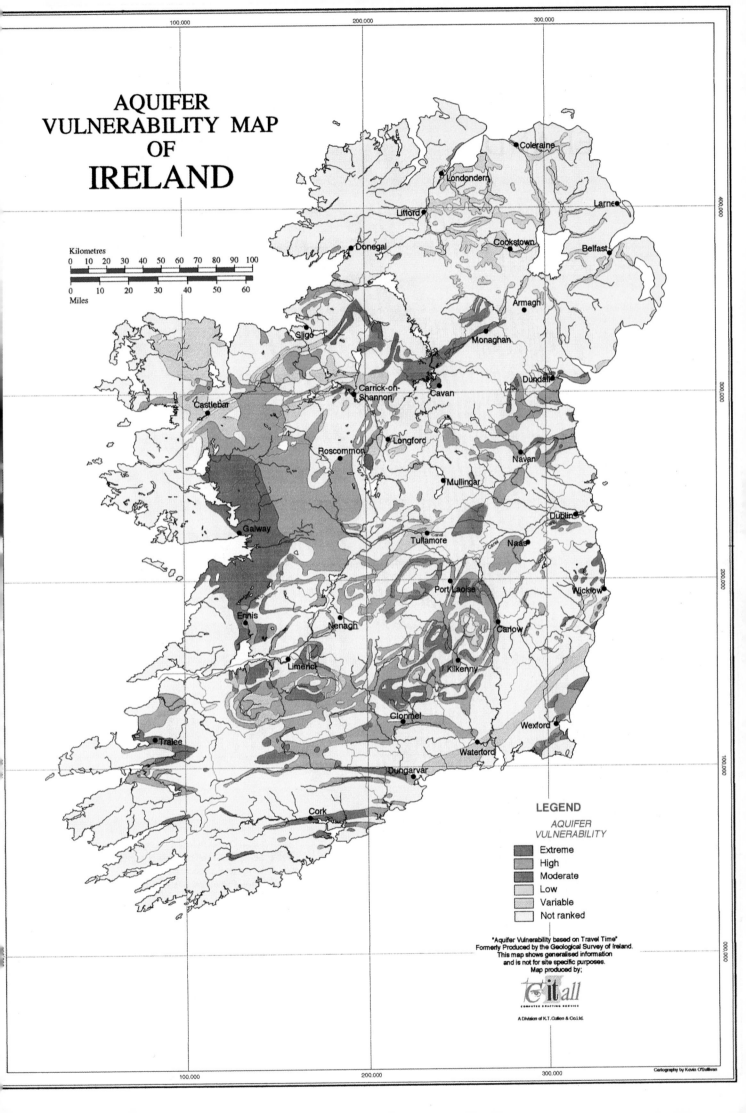

AQUIFER VULNERABILITY MAP OF IRELAND

Kilometres

Miles

LEGEND

AQUIFER VULNERABILITY

- Extreme
- High
- Moderate
- Low
- Variable
- Not ranked

"Aquifer Vulnerability based on Travel Time"
Formerly Produced by the Geological Survey of Ireland.
This map shows generalised information
and is not for site specific purposes.
Map produced by;

A Division of K.T.Cullen & Co.Ltd.

Cartography by Kevin O'Sullivan

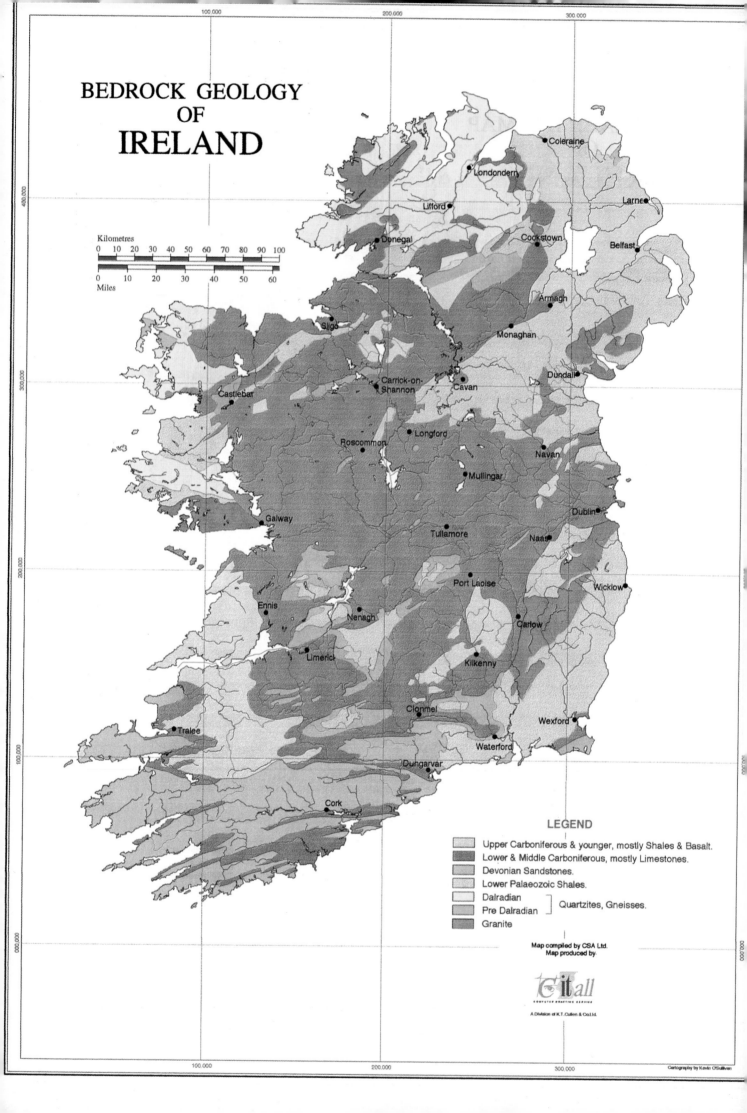

BEDROCK GEOLOGY OF IRELAND

Kilometres
0 10 20 30 40 50 60 70 80 90 100

0 10 20 30 40 50 60
Miles

Coleraine
Londonderry
Larne
Lifford
Donegal
Cookstown
Belfast
Armagh
Sligo
Monaghan
Dundalk
Carrick-on-Shannon
Cavan
Castlebar
Longford
Navan
Roscommon
Mullingar
Galway
Dublin
Tullamore
Naas
Port Laoise
Wicklow
Ennis
Nenagh
Carlow
Limerick
Kilkenny
Clonmel
Wexford
Tralee
Waterford
Dungarvar
Cork

LEGEND

Upper Carboniferous & younger, mostly Shales & Basalt.
Lower & Middle Carboniferous, mostly Limestones.
Devonian Sandstones.
Lower Palaeozoic Shales.
Dalradian
Pre Dalradian] Quartzites, Gneisses.
Granite

Map compiled by CSA Ltd.
Map produced by.

Cit all
COMPUTER DRAFTING SERVICE

A Division of K.T.Cullen & Co.Ltd.

Cartography by Kevin O'Sullivan

Plate 2. Aquifers *(previous pages)*

Deposits of sand and gravel as well as fissured and porous rocks are usually high-yielding aquifers. This map shows the outwash sands and gravels of the Curragh, Co. Kildare, as well as terrace gravels in some river valleys as major aquifers. The most extensive bedrock aquifers are in the coarser, bedded limestones (deposited in deep water) of south central and western counties, followed by the basaltic rocks of the north east. Complex patterns arise from combinations of rock types, structural orientation and the presence or absence of sands and gravels overlying the rocks.

Republished by permission of the Geological Survey of Ireland and K.T. Cullen & Co. Ltd.

Plate 3. Aquifer vulnerability *(previous pages)*

Aquifer vulnerability refers to the ease with which pollutants of various kinds can enter underground water. This property is estimated from the hydraulic conductivity and thickness of the most impermeable layers of soil. This map shows that the most vulnerable aquifers are those underlying thin, loamy soils, such as the brown earths and rendzinas of central Galway and north Clare. Likewise, the sandstone-derived parts of the valleys of Munster do not offer much protection to the underlying aquifers. Where the soil or overburden is thicker, more clayey and/or organic-matter-rich the vulnerability rating is lower.

Republished by permission of the Geological Survey of Ireland and K.T. Cullen & Co. Ltd.

Plate 4. Bedrock geology *(opposite)*

The link between the bedrock geology of Ireland and its agroclimatic environment is mainly through the ability of its rocks to produce weathered products which in turn become productive soils. A productive soil is not necessarily one which gives maximum yields, but rather a versatile and resilient one which can respond to the vagaries in climate, support a range of cropping systems, withstand environmental stresses, act as a biological filter and exchanging mechanism, and so sustain production in the long term.

An equally important link between bedrock and agroclimatology is expressed in the hydrological cycle whereby geological materials act as reservoirs for water, control river flows, dampen watertable fluctuations and provide a dependable supply of fresh water for a whole range of industrial, agricultural and municipal uses.

Simple monochrome maps of bedrock geology are presented on page 27.

Republished by permission of the Geological Survey of Ireland and K.T. Cullen & Co. Ltd.

Synoptic, anemographic and climatological stations

There are fifteen synoptic weather stations in the country. Of these, five are definitely coastal (Belmullet, Malin Head, Rosslare, Roches Point and Valentia); those at the airports (Aldergrove, Cork, Dublin (2) and Shannon) are in coastal counties, while the remaining five (Birr, Claremorris, Clones, Mullingar and Kilkenny) are inland. Synoptic stations are manned by Meteorological Service personnel and make hourly measurements and reports on wind, temperature, pressure, humidity, precipitation, cloud and details of current weather. Hourly sunshine values, daily maximum and minimum temperatures, soil temperatures at several depths, grass-minimum temperatures and observations of the state of the ground (dew, snow, etc.) are also recorded. Some stations carry out additional special observation programmes such as global and diffuse solar radiation measurements and evaporation recording.

Anemograph stations record details of wind speed and direction at 10 m above ground level.

Climatological stations, of which about eighty are currently in operation, supplement the synoptic stations on the basis of measurements taken once daily (at 09:00 h GMT). They are usually maintained by private individuals and institutions interested in climate (Electricity Supply Board, Office of Public Works, Teagasc and teaching institutions). The number of manually-operated stations is likely to decline, though the total number of stations will increase as automatic recording becomes more widely available.

Meteorological Service, Dublin.

Synoptic, anemographic and climatological stations

Meteorologic instrument enclosure

Meteorological stations are located strategically around the country to give us as complete a picture as possible of the national climate; hence the location of individual stations in a locality is important. The fifteen synoptic stations and the much larger number of climatological stations throughout Ireland have enclosures similar to that shown.

The land form should be level and the soil as representative of the local area as possible. It should be placed on level ground away from the influence of trees and buildings and not in a hollow. As indicated, the dimensions are approximately 12m each way. The enclosure should be protected by a post and wire fence 1.2–1.5 m high with a small gate. During establishment an electrical supply for a rain recorder and for automatic instruments should be placed underground. Height above sea level (Ordnance Datum) should be recorded. The ground cover is usually regularly-mown grass.

The usual range of instruments in synoptic and climatological stations is shown. There are usually many variations in the layout to accommodate other arrangements and installations. For example, a number of stations measure potential evapotranspiration and have a bank of three lysimeters with access pits. Kilkenny and Valentia have special equipment for measuring solar radiation (direct, diffuse and reflected). And more and more stations have automatic recorders both at ground level and on masts.

The synoptic stations have a single storey building at the edge of the enclosure in which records and stores are kept as well as facilities for communicating with Head Office. The building usually includes recording devices for many of the outdoor instruments, including an anemometer on the roof. Automatic stations are usually equipped with a tall mast on which several individual recording devices are located. The cabling to the in-house computer should be ducted separately from the electric current to avoid interference.

O'Reilly, G., 1986. Meteorological Elements and their Measurement. Chapter 2 in: Climate, Weather and Irish Agriculture, edited by T. Keane. Agmet Group, Dublin.
Meteorological Office, 1969. Observer's Handbook. Her Majesty's Stationery Office, London.

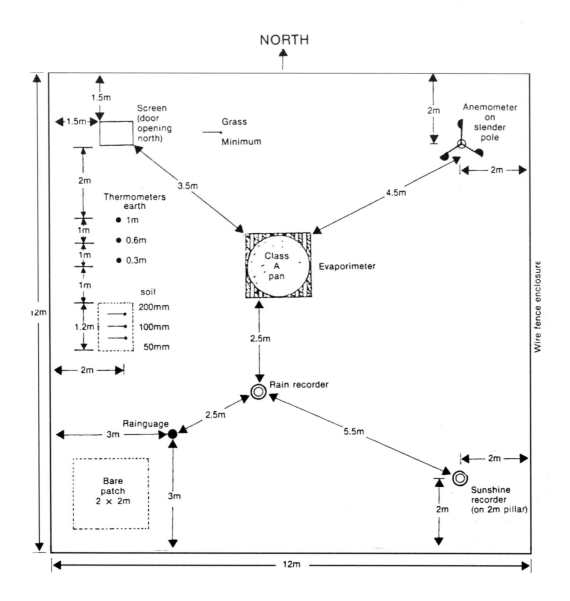

NORTH

Layout of meteorologic instrument enclosure with evaporimeter

Rainfall gauging stations

The standard raingauge used in Ireland collects precipitation falling into its funnel, the upper edge of which is level, bevelled, circular, 127 mm in diameter and 305 mm above the ground level. It is usually made of copper and the rain—and other kinds of precipitation such as hail and snow—received are measured in a specially designed graduated cylinder.

There are about one thousand raingauge sites in the entire island, strategically distributed to give a good over-all cover. The concentration of gauges is greatest in centres of dense population such as Dublin and Belfast. Clusters in Wicklow, on the Sperrins and between Killarney and Kenmare are used to quantify precipitation at high altitudes. The latter gauges are read at monthly intervals generally; the vast majority of the remainder which are maintained by institutions and private individuals are read daily, while those at synoptic stations are read hourly.

The standard raingauges collect less rain than the actual rainfall at that site. The shortfall—which is estimated at about 5%—is due to wind which causes splashing, adhesion and evaporation. The rain equivalent of snow may also be in error due to drifting. Special designs of precipitation gauge for extreme conditions are available, though all give rise to problems when the records are compared to those from standard gauges.

Irish International Committee for the I.H.P., 1982. Hydrology in Ireland. Contribution to the UNESCO International Hydrological Programme, Dublin.

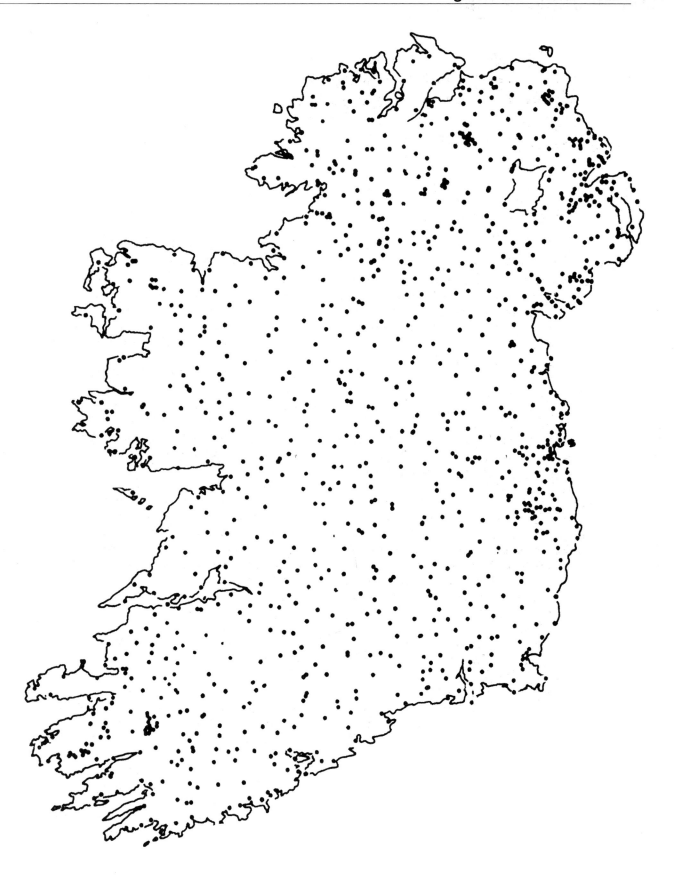

Rainfall gauging stations

Rain recorder stations

Rain recorder stations are stations equipped with autographic rate-of-rainfall recorders. They provide information on the rate at which rain falls or alternatively the maximum amount of rainfall experienced in a short period of time such as an hour. The two main kinds of recorder in use are the tilting siphon and tipping bucket kinds. Both are much larger than the conventional rain gauge and record the amount of water on a chart or electronically.

Rain recorder stations have been installed by the Meteorological Service in accordance with the World Meteorological Organisation (WMO) specifications and are inspected regularly. Most of them are operated by the Meteorological Service itself, by institutions or, in a few cases, by private individuals.

Data from these stations are used, among other things, to design channels and sewers in built up areas, to make predictions as to the likelihood of flash floods or damage to growing crops, the occurrence of capping or erosion in newly cultivated land, and design of surfaces for outdoor sports.

When assessing the rate of rainfall at a point of interest, the geographically nearest station may not be the most suited. It is important to consider topographic features such as altitude and the orientation of hills in order to choose the most comparable station.

Irish International Committee for the I.H.P., 1982. Hydrology in Ireland. Contribution to the UNESCO International Hydrological Programme, Dublin.

Rain recorder stations equipped with autographic recorders, 1982

Evaporimeters and evapotranspirometers

Evaporimeters are devices for measuring the rate of water loss from a free water surface such as a reservoir, lake, pool or saturated soil. Evaporation is of particular interest to the Electricity Supply Board and local authorities (water loss in summer from reservoirs), the Office of Public Works and Regional Fisheries Boards (volume of river flow) and Bord na Mona (rate of drying of peat). The device used for measuring evaporation is a large pan of water, known as a "Class A Pan", fitted with a depth measuring gauge. Evapotranspirometers are devices for measuring the rate of water loss from a short-grass covered surface (such as permanent pasture) adequately supplied with water. Evapotranspirometers are more usually known as lysimeters.

The rate at which water is transpired by plants and evaporated from their leaves, together known as evapotranspiration, is of particular importance to agricultural production and is used in estimating drought and irrigation requirements. Hence most lysimeters are located in research stations, especially those operated by the agricultural research and advisory authority, Teagasc.

Where measured values for evapotranspiration are not available, it is possible to calculate a fairly accurate value by using other meteorological data such as air temperature, relative humidity and wind speed. The best known formula for this purpose is the Penman formula, first published in 1948 and still used today in various modifications.

Irish International Committee for the I.H.P., 1982. Hydrology in Ireland. Contribution to the UNESCO International Hydrological Programme, Dublin.

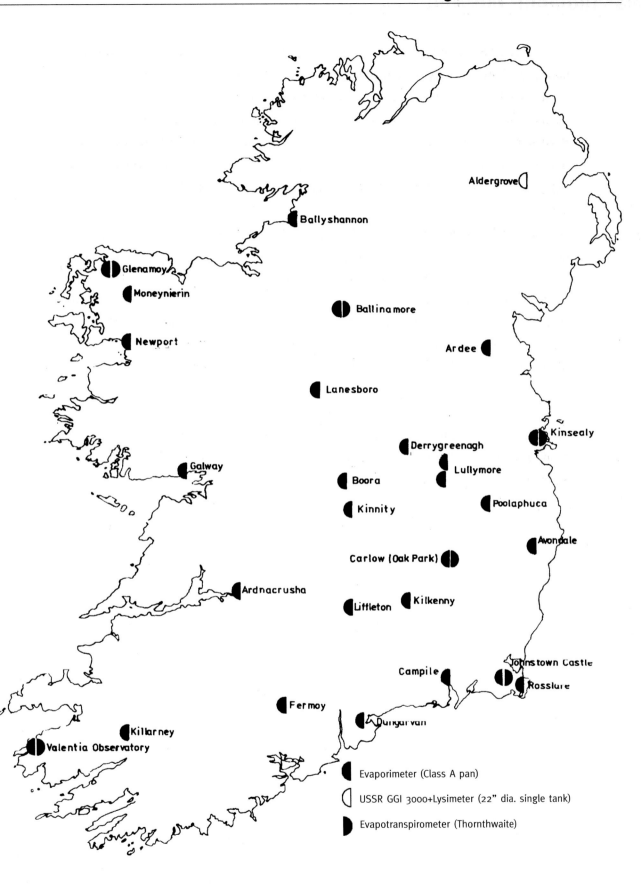

Aldergrove

Ballyshannon

Glenamoy

Moneynierin

Newport

Ballinamore

Ardee

Lanesboro

Kinsealy

Derrygreenagh

Galway

Lullymore

Boora

Poolaphuca

Kinnity

Avondale

Carlow (Oak Park)

Ardnacrusha

Littleton

Kilkenny

Johnstown Castle

Campile

Rosslare

Fermoy

Dungarvan

Killarney

Valentia Observatory

● Evaporimeter (Class A pan)

◖ USSR GGI 3000+Lysimeter (22" dia. single tank)

◗ Evapotranspirometer (Thornthwaite)

Location of stations with evaporimeters and evapotranspirometers

Solar radiation measurement

Seven of the fifteen Irish synoptic stations measure solar radiation incident on a horizontal surface (known as global solar radiation). Six of the seven (Belmullet being the exception) can distinguish between the direct beam (direct radiation) and that which has been scattered and reflected by clouds, aerosols and air molecules (diffuse radiation). Both Kilkenny and Valentia have equipment which distinguishes between total incoming radiation (global) and that reflected by the ground surface, and report the difference as "Net Radiation". In 1995, measurements of ultra-violet radiation started at Valentia.

Data for the duration of sunshine can be used to calculate radiation receipts. Using sunshine and radiation data measured simultaneously over long periods enables good extrapolation of radiation data to be made.

Fitzgerald, Denis, 1992. Climatological Data Archive of the Irish Meteorological Service—an Agricultural Resource?, in: Future of Irish Agriculture—Role of Climate, edited by J.F. Collins. Proceedings of 1992 Agmet Conference, Dublin.

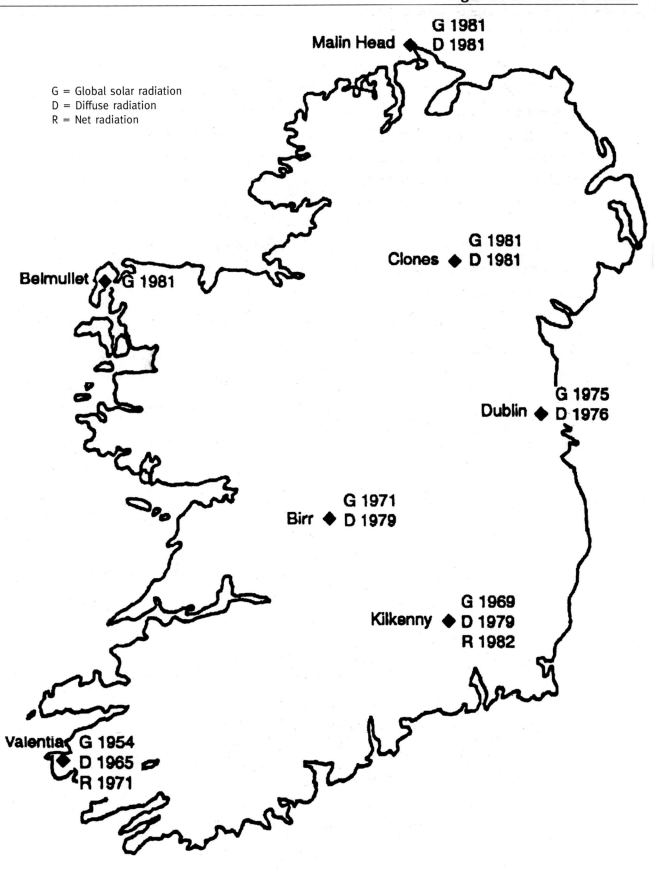

G = Global solar radiation
D = Diffuse radiation
R = Net radiation

G 1981
Malin Head ◆ D 1981

G 1981
Clones ◆ D 1981

Belmullet ◆ G 1981

G 1975
Dublin ◆ D 1976

G 1971
Birr ◆ D 1979

G 1969
Kilkenny ◆ D 1979
R 1982

Valentia G 1954
◆ D 1965
R 1971

Stations where solar radiation is measured (March, 1982).
The year when measurements began is shown for each station

Chemical climate recording

Monitoring chemical climate consists mainly of analysis of bulk precipitation, atmospheric gases and suspended atmospheric solids. Bulk precipitation samples are usually collected in a plastic funnel apparatus similar to a standard copper rain gauge. Suspended solids are usually collected using air drawn through filters, and the filtered particles washed into solution for analysis. Gas analysis can be made on air samples themselves, or on samples of gas deposited onto specific absorbing surfaces.

The stations shown on this map have all carried out collection of precipitation samples for chemical analysis over several years. Many have also monitored atmospheric gases or particles or both. Many other observations of chemical weather have been made throughout Ireland, though generally for shorter periods. There are also country-wide networks monitoring sulphur dioxide and tropospheric ozone, and urban–area networks measuring carbon monoxide and smoke, among others. The Meteorological Service's synoptic stations have the longest continuous records of precipitation and air chemistry. The Valentia Station measures total ozone column and tropospheric ozone and makes ozonesonde balloon ascents. Long-term background measurements of gaseous species have also been made at the Mace Head site, operated by University College Galway's Atmospheric Physics Research Group.

Since threats to health or economic activities from chemical weather have generally not been very serious, monitoring of chemical climates has not been given the same attention in Ireland or worldwide as have physical climates. This situation is now changing, with the first public information announcements on ozone levels given during the hot summer of 1995.

Meteorological Service synoptic stations: Malin Head, Clones, Dublin Airport, Birr, Rosslare, Cork Airport, Valentia, Shannon, Belmullet.
Environmental Protection Agency, formerly Environmental Research Unit, Department of the Environment: Doo Lough, Glencree, Glenveagh, Gortglass, Maam Valley, Radestown, Turlough Hill.
University College Dublin, Forest Ecosystem Research Group: Ballyhooly, Brackloon, Cloosh, Roundwood.
Northern Ireland Freshwater Biological Investigations Unit: Altnaheglish, Fourmile Burn, Silent Valley.
Electricity Supply Board: Burren, Slieve Bloom.
University College Galway, Atmospheric Physics Research Group: Mace Head.
Northern Ireland Fisheries Service: Lough Navar.

J. Aherne (Private Communications) Forest Ecosystem Research Group, University College, Dublin.

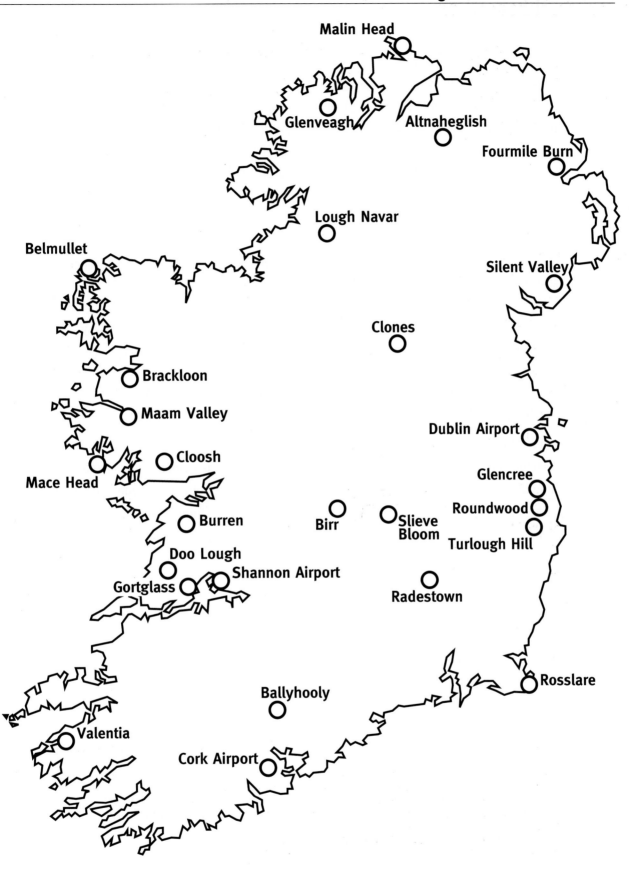

Malin Head

Glenveagh

Altnaheglish

Fourmile Burn

Lough Navar

Silent Valley

Belmullet

Clones

Brackloon

Maam Valley

Dublin Airport

Cloosh

Glencree

Roundwood

Mace Head

Burren

Birr

Slieve Bloom

Turlough Hill

Doo Lough

Shannon Airport

Gortglass

Radestown

Rosslare

Ballyhooly

Valentia

Cork Airport

Some stations where precipitation has been collected for chemical analysis and other chemical climate measurements have been made

Water level recording

Water-flow- and water-level-measurement in this country are relatively recent. Prior to 1960, manually read gauges gave an estimate of flow in some of the main rivers. The number of measuring points (gauging stations) numbered about 1000 in the early 1980s and about 1400 in 1993. The gauging locations include main arteries, tributaries, tidal sections and lakes. The principal hydrological agencies which operate the gauges are the Office of Public Works, local authorities and the Electricity Supply Board, and more recently the Environmental Protection Agency.

Gauge data are used for planning abstraction potentials, weir, bridge and culvert design, effluent dilution, quality monitoring methods, drainage and flood relief schemes and the impacts of development on surface- and groundwaters.

The kinds of automatic recorders in use have improved with advancing technology. Charts were replaced by punched tape and transmitting type recorders, and some have remote interrogation recorders coupled to the telephone system.

Since only a small proportion of the municipal water we use is taken from groundwater reserves, measurement of groundwater levels is fairly recent and confined to selected catchments. The responsibility for groundwater measurement rests mainly with Groundwater Division of the Geological Survey of Ireland. Automatic recorders are gradually replacing measured dipping of wells. Pumping tests from wells and boreholes allow investigators to identify local aquifers and assess the relative rates of recharge.

Environmental Protection Agency, 1995. Hydrological Data A listing of water level recorders and summary statistics at selected gauging stations.
Irish International Committee for the I.H.P., 1982. Hydrology in Ireland. Contribution to the UNESCO International Hydrological Programme, Dublin.

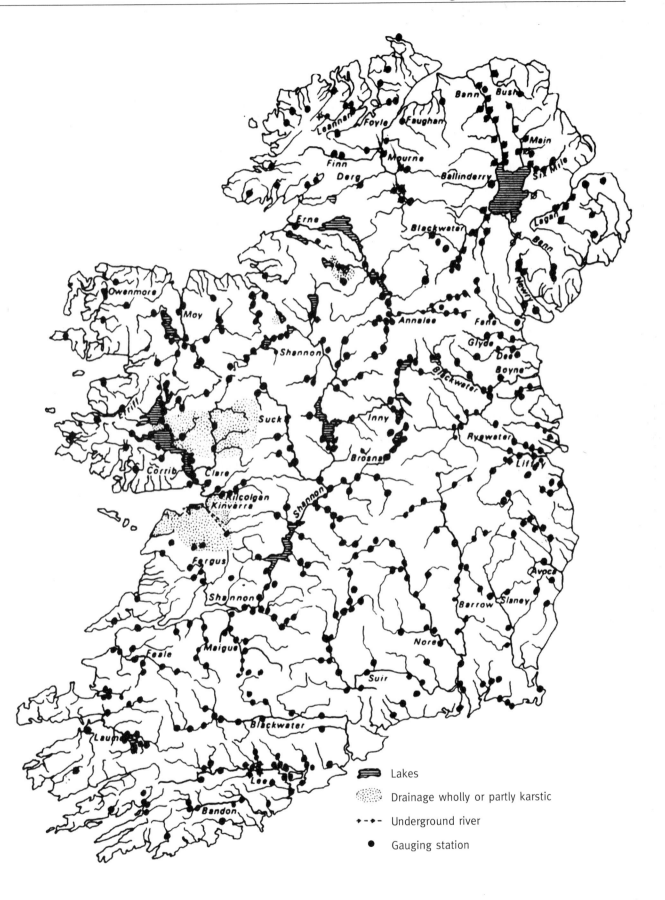

Rivers, lakes and tidal zones with water-level gauging stations

Meteorology and hydrology are closely related sciences and both have water as the main focus of their interests. That portion of the water receipts (precipitation) that runs off the land surface or seeps underground determines how much water will go into river flow, the fluctuation in groundwater levels and the reserves available for a wide variety of uses. Hydrometeorology is a study of volumes and rates at which that water is available and is usually divided into surface flow and groundwater fluctuations. This map shows hydrometric areas numbered 1–40, each of which comprises a single large river basin or a group of smaller ones. Each has a number, a name and a description, for example: "07, Boyne; the surface catchment drained by the river Boyne and all streams entering tidal water between the Haven, Co. Louth and Mornington Point, Co. Meath".

Water resource regions are groups of adjoining hydrometric areas and each has a regional geographic name such as "southern". These regions are more uniform in size range (mid-western, 7640 km^2–southeastern, 12,790 km^2) and have been used over the years as the basis for assessment of water resources.

Knowledge of river and lake levels, flows, discharge and recharge rates, as well as chemical and biological condition of waters has implications for agriculture that range from flood- and drought-hazard to dilution of potential pollutants to spread of diseases, and from angling to the location of industrial installations.

Environmental Protection Agency, 1995. Hydrological Data A listing of water level recorders and summary statistics at selected gauging stations.

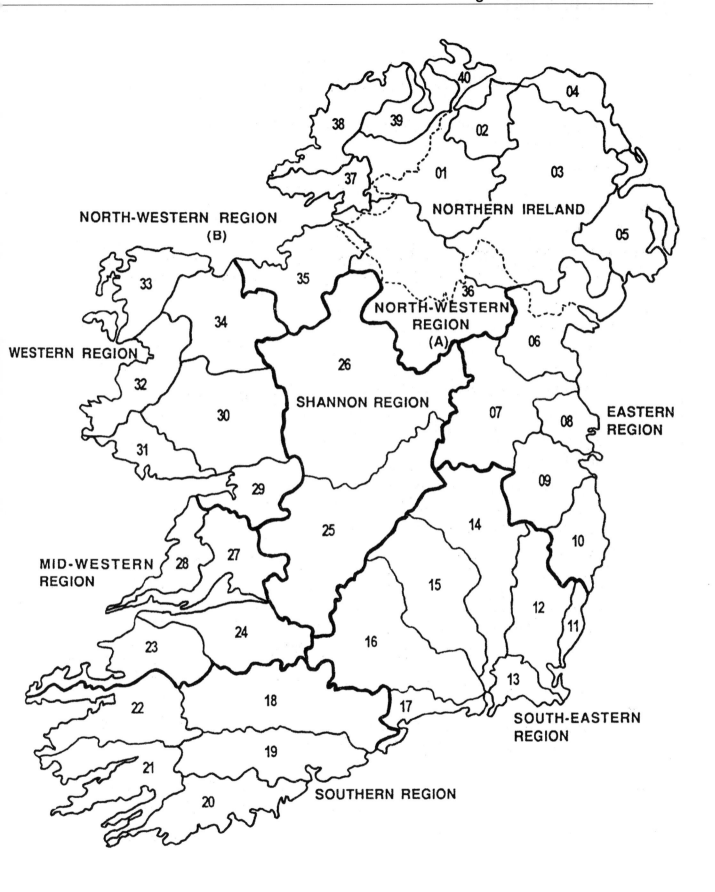

NORTH-WESTERN REGION
(B)

WESTERN REGION

NORTHERN IRELAND

NORTH-WESTERN
REGION
(A)

EASTERN
REGION

SHANNON REGION

MID-WESTERN
REGION

SOUTH-EASTERN
REGION

SOUTHERN REGION

Water resource regions and hydrometric areas

Sea area forecasts

Those who listen to sea area forecasts on radio will be familiar with the names of a variety of headlands, promontories, loughs and lighthouses around the coast. These help to divide a strip of coastal waters about 35 miles (56 km) wide in the Irish Sea, Celtic Sea and Atlantic ocean so that ships, boats and other craft can receive a fairly accurate forecast for their location.

The standard forecast includes the meteorological or synoptic situation and weather for named regions of Irish coastal waters and the Irish Sea. The general situation is described in terms such as depressions, anticyclones and troughs, expected in the following 24 hours; weather terms include fine, fair, cloudy, mist and haze; wind speed is given in terms of the Beaufort scale or in miles per hour; there are four terms used for describing visibility: good (>9 km), moderate (4–9 km), poor (1–4 km) and fog (<1000 m).

A brief outlook for the 24-hour period following the detailed forecast period is given, followed by reports from six stations in the following order: Malin Head, Rosslare, Roches Point, Valentia and Belmullet, finishing with the report form Dublin Airport. The coastal reports give wind, weather, visibility, pressure and pressure tendency. Gale warnings are issued if winds of Beaufort Force eight or more are expected. A table showing the Beaufort wind force scale is given in an appendix.

BBC shipping forecasts divide the waters around Britain and Ireland and a large area of the northeast Atlantic into twenty eight areas. The forecasts deal with them in a clockwise direction starting with "Viking" near Norway and ending with "Southeast Iceland".

An Atlantic Weather Bulletin covers a still larger area, as far west as the 45th meridian (45°W) and between the latitudes of North Africa and Greenland.

Meteorological Service, Dublin.

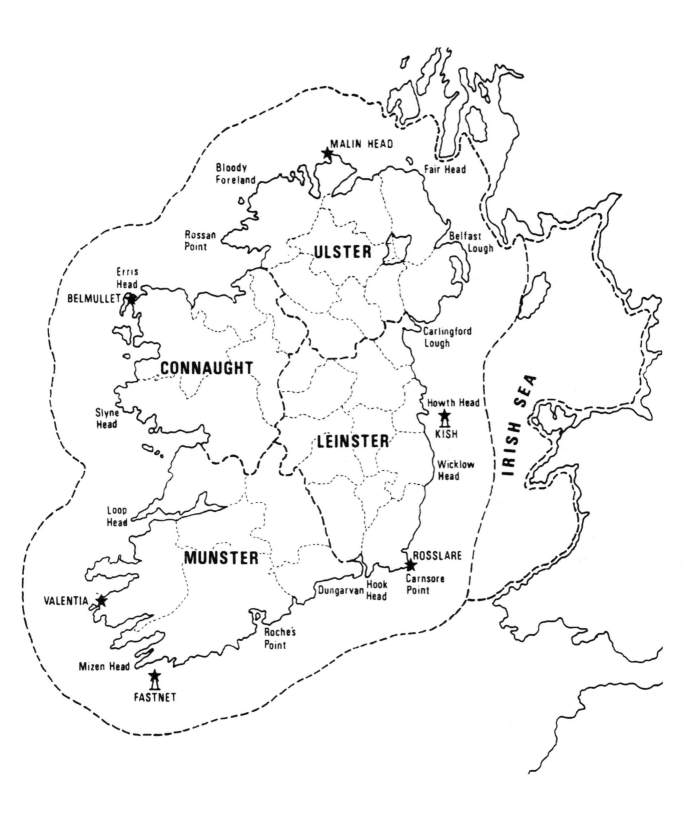

Headlands, inlets and stations referred to in the forecasts for coastal waters and the Irish Sea given by the Irish Meteorological Service

Radar detection of precipitation

Weather radar allows precipitation to be detected and measured over a wide area. The radar sends out pulses, a portion of which are reflected back to the radar by precipitation. The echo signal received is related to the reflectivity of the precipitation, and hence to the precipitation rate (mm/hour).

Radars can scan a region of up to 240 km diameter (outer light shaded ranges in this map) giving useful information on the location and intensity of precipitation. However, accurate estimates can only be made within ranges of about 100 km (inner dark shaded areas). At longer ranges the errors become too large for meaningful results.

There are three weather radars in Ireland, at Dublin and Shannon Airports, and at Castor Bay in Northern Ireland. Data from all three contribute to a UK–Ireland and European composite which is seen on the television weather forecasts.

Weather radar data can be used for computing total rainfall accumulations over large areas such as river basins. Such data are increasingly used for flood prediction, water supply and irrigation management.

Meteorological Service, Dublin.

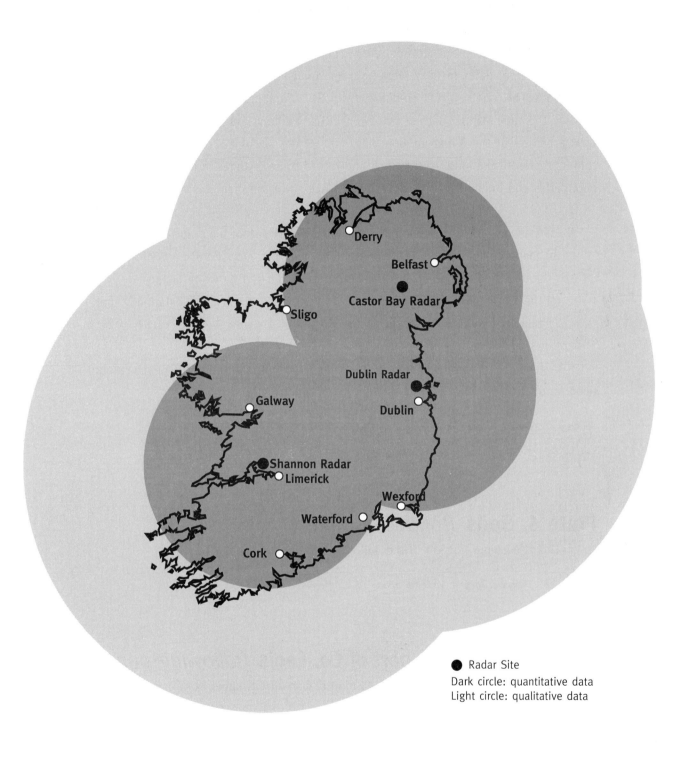

Weather radar coverage giving quantitative (inner zones) and qualitative (outer zones) detection of precipitation

Plate 5. Satellite image superimposed on the six-inch scale (1:10,560) map of a small area south of Castledermot, Co. Kildare. *(opposite)*

This image was produced from data acquired from three different satellite sensors on three different dates in 1993. Data from the pan-chromatic sensor of the SPOT satellite acquired on April 29 was combined with SPOT multispectral data for May 7 and Landsat Thematic Mapper data of October 17. The resultant image was overlain with the 1906/7 edition of the 6-inch to one mile map (Sheet 40 of Co. Kildare). The various colours represent the land uses in 1993 and record some changes in crop type and field boundaries and buildings which have taken place since the map was made, such as:

(a) the wood shown lower left has been removed except for the purple-coloured area;

(b) the large field (under OCKN of Knocknacree) is composed of parts or all of six former fields (fences on the six-inch map indicated by white lines);

(c) the large reflections around most of the houses indicate substantially more buildings than were shown on the map.

In general, the various shades of green represent grassland and the peach colours tilled land.

Courtesy of University College Dublin Remote Sensing Laboratory;
Ordnance Survey of Ireland, Pheonix Park, Dublin.

Plate 6. Soils *(following pages)*

This is a colour version of the soil map presented on page 41.

Courtesy of S. Diamond, Teagasc, Wexford.

Plate 7. Soil series, part of Co. Laois *(following pages)*

This is a colour version of the soil map of part of Co. Laois from page 47.

Courtesy of S. Diamond, Teagasc, Wexford.

Satellite image/six-inch map overlay

Soils

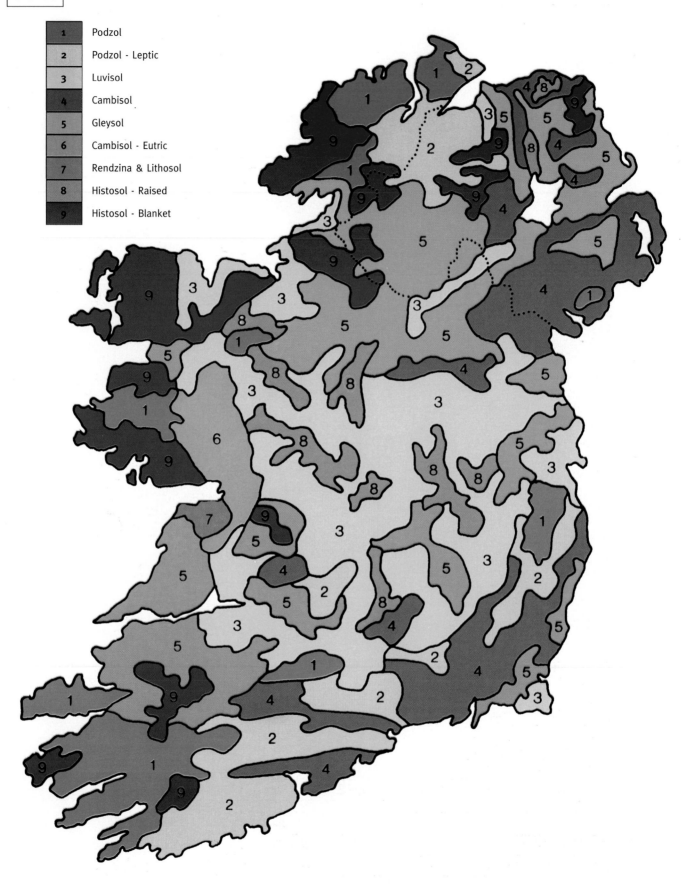

1	Podzol
2	Podzol - Leptic
3	Luvisol
4	Cambisol
5	Gleysol
6	Cambisol - Eutric
7	Rendzina & Lithosol
8	Histosol - Raised
9	Histosol - Blanket

Soil series, part of Co. Laois

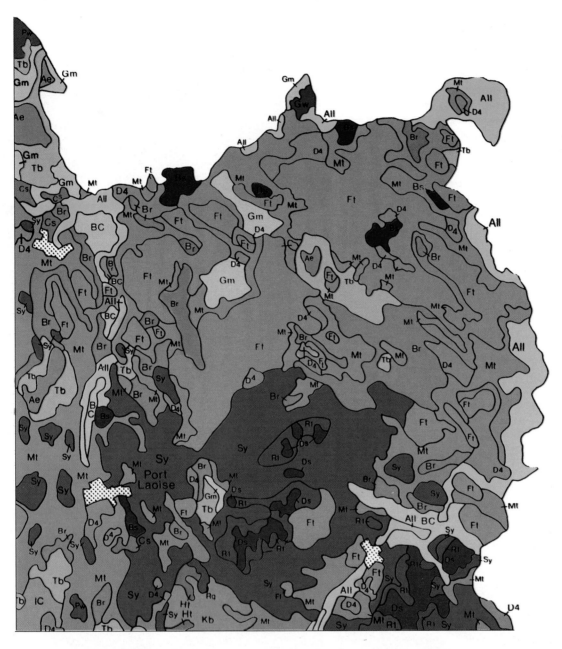

Great Soil Group	Brown Earth	Grey Brown Podzolic				
	Rg	Sy	R1	Ft	Kb	
Soil Series	Ridge	Stradbally	Rocky phase	Fontstown	Knockbeg	Patrickswell

Complex	Podzol-Grey Br. Podzolic	Gley				
All	Gw	Mt	D4	Bs	Ht	Cs
Alluvium	Gracewell	Mylerstown	Imperfectly Drained phase	Ballyshear	Howardstown	Clonaslee

Complex		Peat				
BC	Ds	Br	Gm	Tb	Ae	IC
Baggottstown Carlow	Dysart Hills	Banagher	Gortnamona	Turbary Complex	Allen	Industrial Complex

Runoff risk categories for soils

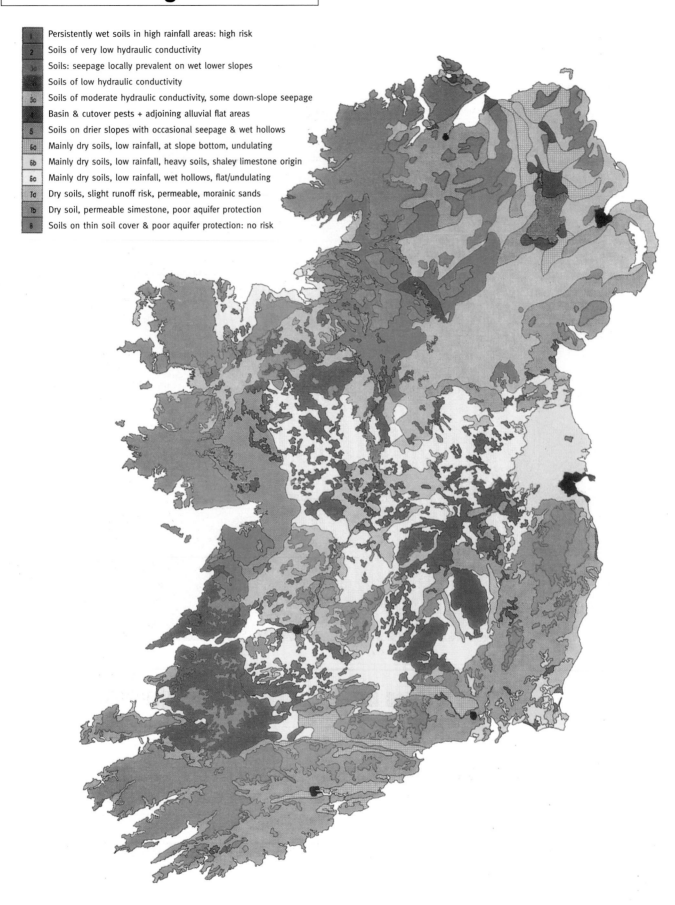

1	Persistently wet soils in high rainfall areas: high risk
2	Soils of very low hydraulic conductivity
3a	Soils: seepage locally prevalent on wet lower slopes
3b	Soils of low hydraulic conductivity
3c	Soils of moderate hydraulic conductivity, some down-slope seepage
4	Basin & cutover pests + adjoining alluvial flat areas
5	Soils on drier slopes with occasional seepage & wet hollows
6a	Mainly dry soils, low rainfall, at slope bottom, undulating
6b	Mainly dry soils, low rainfall, heavy soils, shaley limestone origin
6c	Mainly dry soils, low rainfall, wet hollows, flat/undulating
7a	Dry soils, slight runoff risk, permeable, morainic sands
7b	Dry soil, permeable simestone, poor aquifer protection
8	Soils on thin soil cover & poor aquifer protection: no risk

CLASSIFICATION BY TIM GLEESON, SOIL PHYSICS LAB, KINSEALY.

(C) COPYRIGHT TEAGASC 1992

PLOTS SUPPLIED BY QC-DATA CORK

Teagasc

Johnstown Castle, Wexford

Plate 8. Runoff risks of Irish soils *(opposite)*

Two major properties of soils are their abilities to absorb and retain water for plant growth and the ability to transmit water downwards, eventually recharging the groundwater. Another pathway by which water may leave the surface it falls on is as surface runoff laterally. This overland pathway may be due to saturation excess or infiltration excess. Saturation excess occurs when soil pores are already filled with water; infiltration excess is much less common, occurring only when the soil cannot imbibe the water at the rate at which it is falling. Infiltration excess can be a problem on soils which are damaged through compaction, caking or slaking—paths and goalmouths, for example.

Until recently, runoff was a worry only when it contributed to flooding, causing damage to gullies, culverts and other engineering installations. Nowadays all those dealing with land and water resources are concerned with runoff since it may bring with it soluble and suspended material from the land surface and thereby potentially pollute waterways.

This map shows the soils of Ireland placed in eight categories (with some subcategories) of runoff risk. The categories are based on the nature and properties of the soil (depth, texture, structure, hydraulic conductivity, stoniness etc.), site characteristics (slope, vegetation etc.) and rainfall (intensity, amount).

The soils giving the highest risk (class 1) are those that are persistently wet (blanket peats, peaty podzols) together with bare, non-porous rocks on steep slopes. At the other end of the scale (class 8), runoff is least likely on very permeable sands and gravels, and shallow soils over fissured and porous rock. Many of the soils of the drumlin region have low hydraulic conductivity and are placed in classes 2 and 3. Many of the better areas of agricultural land (both tillage and pasture) are in classes 5 and 6.

As with all maps, the limitations of scale must be taken into account. Categories of different risk can occur on the same farm. Especially note that in those areas where runoff-risk is lowest, the risks of pollution of groundwater are often highest.

Anon, 1992. Runoff Risk of Irish Soils. Chapter 4 in: Weather, Soils and Pollution from Agriculture, compiled by M. Sherwood. Agmet Group, Dublin. Original compiled by T. Gleeson, Teagasc, Kinsealy, Co. Dublin.

Precipitation (rainfall)

Rainfall is one of our most variable meteorological parameters. While the 1000 mm annual isohyet divides the country fairly evenly in two, the western half has a much more variable precipitation, and totals as much as 2–3 times those of the eastern part. Much of the variation is due to hills and mountains and the position of high land in Counties Cork, Kerry, Galway, Mayo and Donegal can be easily picked out on this map. The annual average rainfall in the lowlands of all provinces varies from about 750 mm in the Louth–Dublin area to around 1200 mm in the west, northwest and southeast. As well as Dublin, most of the urban areas (Derry, Belfast, Armagh, Kilkenny, Waterford, Cork and Limerick) and their immediate hinterlands are situated in areas receiving no more than about 1000 mm annually on average.

The orographic rainfall in the uplands causes rainshadows downwind. While not as extreme as in other countries, examples evident in this map show parts of Kildare and Laois in the shadow of the Castlecomer Plateau and Slieve Bloom Mountains, the Dublin–Meath–Louth coasts protected from southerly airflows and the Strangford Lough region in the shadow of the Mournes.

Year to year variability in precipitation is fairly substantial, with some years living on in the memory as very dry or very wet years. While the statistics show a standard deviation of 10–13% for most stations, it is also recorded that the wettest and driest years do not coincide for all stations.

98

Louge, J.J., 1995 (reprint) Extreme rainfalls in Ireland Technical Note No. 40. Meteorological Service, Dublin.

Mean annual precipitation, mm/year, 1951–1980

Monthly precipitation

The bar graphs overlain on this map show the mean monthly rainfall at strategic positions around the country. While nearly all locations receive on average 50 mm every month, some regularly receive over 100 mm in many months and a few western stations receive over 150 mm in some winter months. Even though it is not very distinctive or well defined, the five months of February to June are generally drier than the remaining seven months. February is distinctly drier than January at all stations, on average, but more so in the west. The return to wet weather in the autumn is more gradual. In the southern regions, particularly Counties Cork and Kerry, warm season rain (May–October) contributes relatively less to the yearly total, whereas in the midlands and northeast a greater proportion of the rainfall occurs during this period (compare July values for Cork with Armagh: Cork ~70 mm, Armagh, ~90 mm). One of the agricultural implications of a dry period starting in February is that land is given an opportunity to dry out after the wet winter period; drying will allow soil temperatures to increase quicker than if the soil remained wet, and hence agricultural activities such as fertilizer applications, cultivations and grazing can go ahead.

The actual variation from month to month in any year is much greater than these mean values show.

Meteorological Service, Dublin.

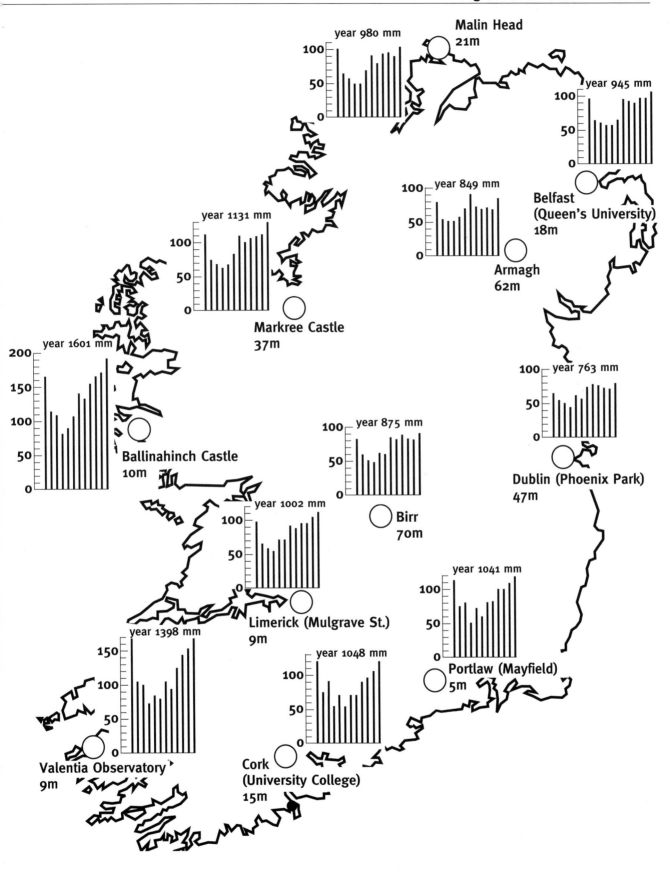

Mean monthly precipitation, mm/month, at selected stations, 1931–1960

Air-mass circulation and rainfall

Hubert Lamb categorised the airflow affecting Britain and Ireland into seven primary weather types: anticyclonic, cyclonic, northwesterly, westerly, northerly, easterly and southerly. The mean precipitation delivered by days of each primary type is shown in this group of eight maps. Typical weather patterns associated with these airflow types are described below. Many weather systems are hybrids of two or more primary airflow types, and show intermediate properties.

Northerly: a northerly airflow gives more rain along the north Ulster and north Connaght coasts with a rain shadow to the lee of the Mourne and Wicklow mountains; cold, disturbed weather at all seasons, especially in east and north; snow and sleet are common in winter; also associated with late-spring frosts.

Easterly: a fairly rare event (3.5% of the synoptic situations analysed); cold in autumn, winter and spring; warm in summer, sometimes thundery; fine and dry in the west and north-west, relatively dry elsewhere, except in the south and east.

Anticyclonic: high pressure; mainly dry with light winds; usually warm in summer and cold or very cold in winter; mist and fog are frequent in autumn with this type.

Cyclonic: low pressure; mainly wet or disturbed weather, with very variable wind directions and strengths; usually mild in autumn and early winter, cool or cold in spring, summer and (sometimes) in late winter; gales and thunderstorms occur.

Southerly: warm and thundery in spring and summer, mild in autumn; in winter it is mild or cold according as the air mass carried over Ireland is oceanic or continental in origin; intense orographic rainfall over the southern mountains.

Westerly: generally unsettled or changeable weather; winds veering rapidly from south-east or south to northwest; cool in summer, mild in winter with frequent gales; high frequency (18.9%) causing a west-to-east precipitation gradient, pronounced higher values in the mountains and distinct rain shadows downwind.

Northwesterly: unsettled, changeable weather, especially in north and east, sometimes with fresh or gale-force winds from between west and north; the warm sectors may contain unstable air, especially in late winter and spring; a distinct general northwest–southeast decrease in rainfall, and a more local trend in west Munster.

The air-mass circulation types last for periods of a few days to a few weeks, and shorter-term variations occur within periods of each type. For example, in a westerly spell, winds over Ireland will veer from southerly to northwesterly as depression centres pass eastwards to our north.

Sweeney, J.C., 1994. Climate scenarios for Ireland, in: Climate Variation and Climate Change in Ireland, edited by J. Feehan. Environmental Institute, University College, Dublin.

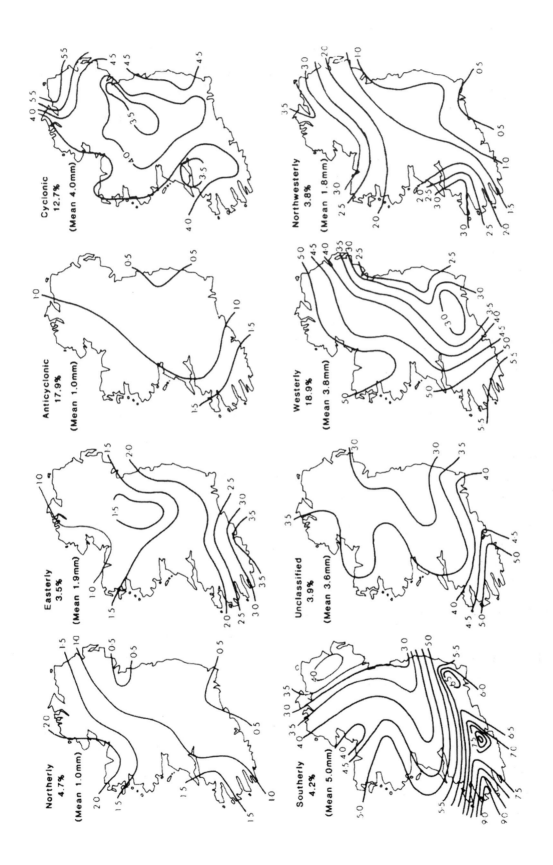

Mean daily precipitation yield, mm, for days classified in principal Lamb synoptic circulation categories

The belief that in the west of Ireland "it rains five days out of seven and threatens to rain on the other two" is not entirely quashed by this map. Three out of five is near the mark for some of the higher altitudes. The caption reads "equal to or more than 1 mm" per day—that is the accepted meteorological definition of a "wet day". There is a fairly obvious southeast–northwest trend for the lowlands and an altitudinal trend in the mountainous and hilly areas. An associated meteorological parameter is "rain-day"—a term relating to a rainfall of not less than 0.2 mm in a 24-hour period. The consequences of such days or runs of such days depend on the time of year, the greater numbers occurring in the December–January period and the least in June–July. May has the highest year-to-year variation in the number of rain-days in the month, which reduces Ireland's suitability for crops which require a wet spring, or those needing a dry spring.

A period of fifteen or more consecutive wet-days is known as a wet spell—a rare enough event, especially in eastern counties.

Rohan, P.K., 1975. The Climate of Ireland. The Stationery Office, Dublin.

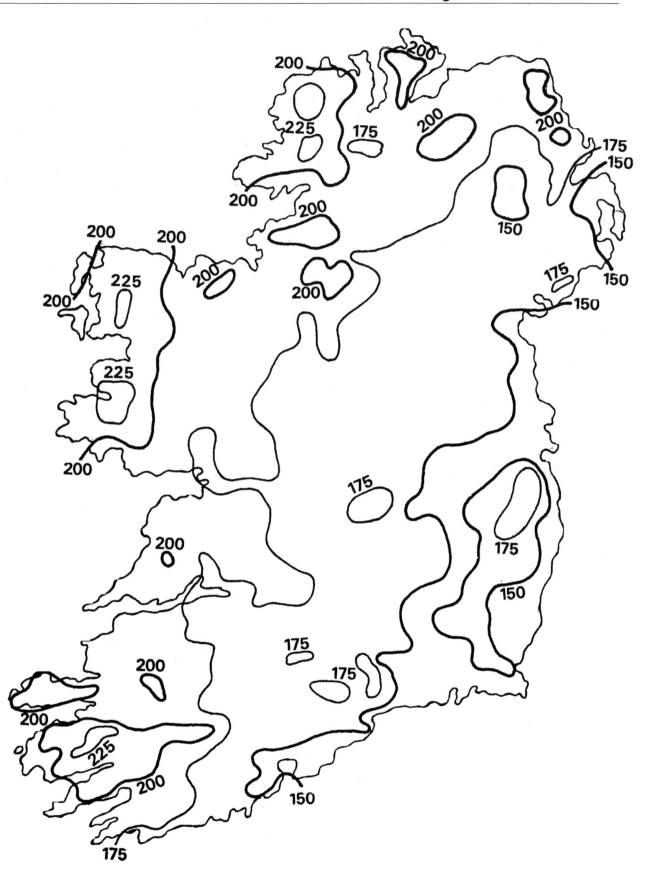

Mean annual number of days having rainfall equal to or more than 1 mm, 1941–1960

Very wet days

Even though the number per year may not be changing, the occurrence of days with high or very high rainfall amounts is becoming of more interest to many people. While planners, engineers and others need to know about flooding, damage to property and even injury and death, a knowledge of the likelihood of days with 5, 10, 15 or more millimetres of rain in a day is needed by those who manage and monitor runoff from land and pollution of water. This graph shows the annual frequency of days with rainfall amounts ranging as high as 30 mm for four representative stations in Ireland. A value of 10 mm of rainfall or more has been used to define the standard "very wet day"; the graph shows that the number of such occasions annually ranges between averages of 45 at Valentia (Cahirciveen), 31 at Claremorris and 22 at Clones and Kilkenny. Long-term records collected by the Meteorological Service show that Delphi Lodge in West Mayo is amongst the highest in this scale with 88 days and Casement Aerodrome (near Dublin) the lowest with a mere 17 very wet days per year on average. In the period 1960 to 1984, 10 mm of precipitation or more fell at least once in every month on average at 26 representative stations and on ten days on average (in the 24 years) in each of the months October to January at Delphi Lodge, Co. Mayo.

Anon., 1992. Meteorological Conditions and Runoff. Chapter 5 in: Soils, Weather and Pollution from Agriculture, compiled by M. Sherwood. Agmet Group, Dublin.

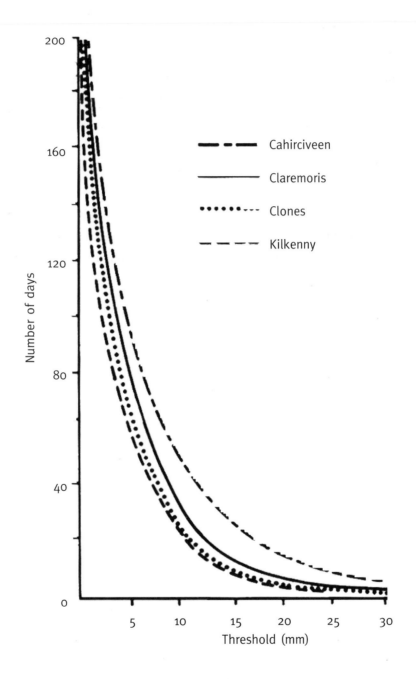

Annual frequency of occurrence of days with rainfall of varying threshold values (ranging from 0.2 mm to 30 mm) at Cahirciveen (Valentia), Claremorris, Clones and Kilkenny.

Extreme rainfall events

Information on the frequency of heavy rainfalls is often required by agriculturists, environmentalists, engineers, architects and others. They are most needed in connection with design criteria for water management and drainage schemes. In most cases it would be uneconomic to construct systems capable of coping with the most extreme rainfall possible, even if the magnitude of this were known. Instead, it is usual to design a system which will be capable of accommodating a rainfall likely to be exceeded only once in a specified period of time. This specified period is known as the return period. The longer the return period, the greater the magnitude of the rainfall event for which allowance can be made. The duration of the rainfall event which is of interest depends on the characteristics and properties of the receiving area and the use to which the peak-flow information is to be put.

The basis for making calculations about frequency of certain events is a historical sequence for a number of years. A period of 25–30 years is commonly regarded as adequate for most predictions, but in order to make confident statements for longer periods, data from a number of stations having similar characteristics and located in the same climatic region are necessary. By statistically analysing the data, maps can be constructed for various combinations of rainfall amounts and return periods.

These maps show expected rainfall amounts in mm, with a return period of 5 years. Any combination of rainfall amount and return period from 1 hour to 1 calendar month can be similarly constructed. The shorter periods, for example 1 hour or 2 hours, are of interest in the design of facilities in a small area, for example drainage of a football field or a cattle yard; intermediate values (1 day, 2 days, 5 days) are used in designing the spacing of mole drains for poorly-permeable land, while larger values come into play when designing more permanent structures serving larger catchments, such as culverts, bridges and arterial drainage schemes.

Logue, J.J., reprint 1995. Extreme Rainfalls in Ireland. Technical Note No. 40. Meteorological Service, Dublin.

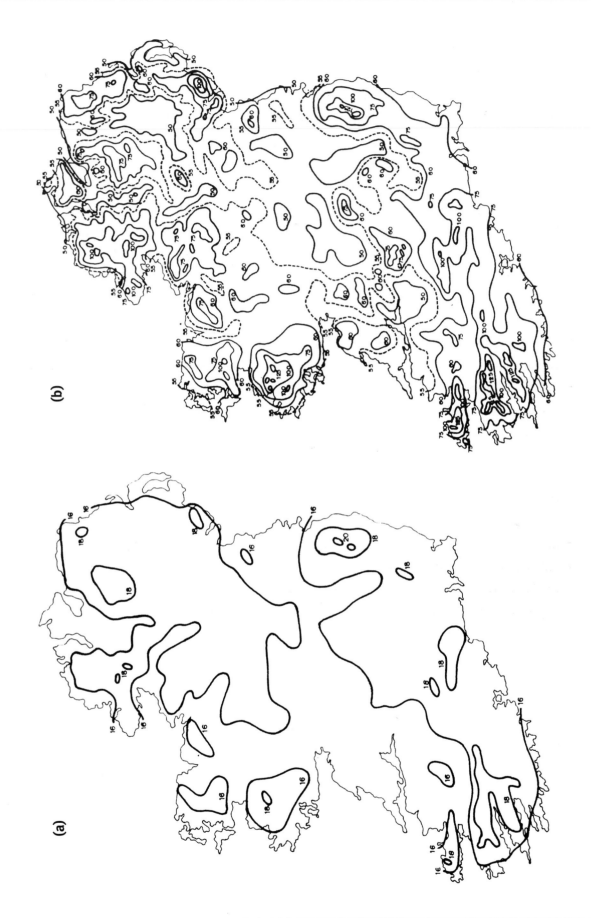

(b)

(a)

Rainfall amounts, mm, with a return period of five years, for times of (a) sixty minutes and (b) two days

Mean air temperature and daily range

Air temperature at synoptic stations is measured continually and/or read hourly from thermometers and thermographs located in Stevenson screens. The height of these above ground level is 1.2 m, and the temperature recorded in these screens is referred to as "air temperature". Where hourly values are measured, they can be averaged over the 365–366 days of the year. Apart from the synoptic stations, daily maximum and minimum temperatures are generally all that are available, and the daily mean is estimated as the mean of these two measurements for each day. Over extended periods, this method comes very close to giving the true mean of more continuous measurements. The long-term mean, if available, is the mean of thirty years' measurements, for a period between years which are multiples of thirty. The recording period shown here is 1951–1980, though the most recent standard period in the World Meteorological Organisation system is 1961–1990.

It is usual to make an adjustment of the data since the stations vary in altitude, so the mean values are "reduced to mean sea level". The 10°C isohyet passes through much of Leinster and Munster, and parts of Connaught. Inland and upland areas in east central Ulster are one degree colder on average while much of southern Munster is half a degree warmer. The coastal influence is evident, as is the "heat island" in the Dublin city area (page 121).

Map (b) shows that the difference between the mean daily maximum (usually afternoon) and mean daily minimum (often just before dawn) temperatures are greatest (8°C) in south Munster and central Leinster, and that the smallest mean difference (5°C) is confined to the coastal extremities of Donegal. This map emphasises the difference in heat capacity between soil/mineral matter and the ocean surface, especially that of the Atlantic which is influenced by the North Atlantic Drift.

Rohan, P.K., 1986. The Climate of Ireland. The Stationery Office, Dublin.

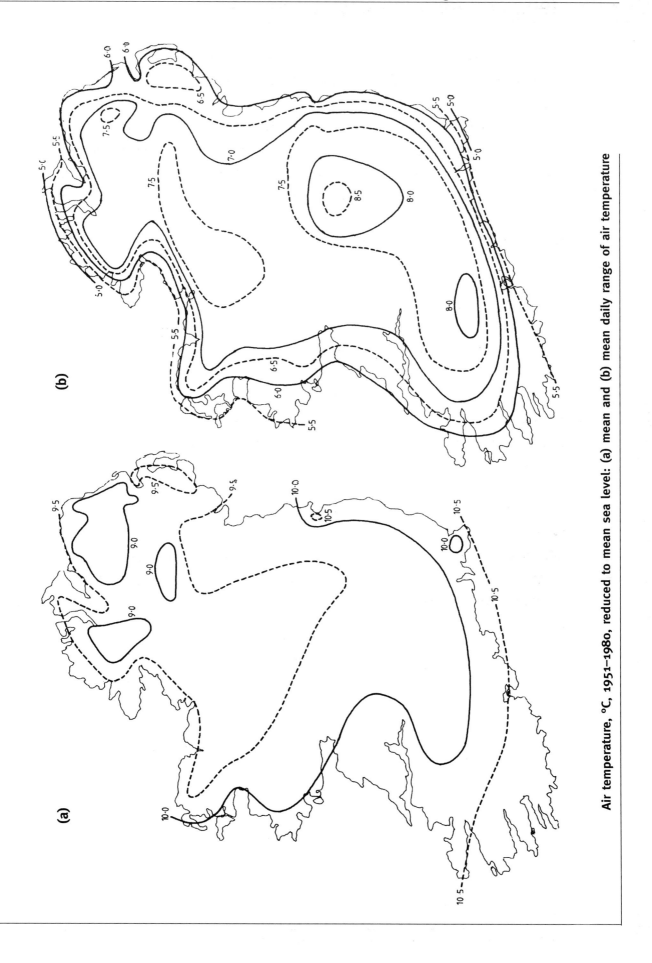

Air temperature, °C, 1951–1980, reduced to mean sea level: (a) mean and (b) mean daily range of air temperature

January and July mean daily air temperatures

Even though days are shortest in December and longest in June and, correspondingly, radiation receipts are least and greatest in the same months, extremes of mean daily temperatures occur in January and July. This delay or time lag is known as a lapse period. Air temperatures are governed mainly by convection from underlying surfaces (water, soil, rock) and these bodies continue to warm up and cool down until the heat they receive and give out are in balance.

The January average for the country approximates 5°C while the long-term July mean is a little over 15°C. Both maps show a latitudinal trend from south to north, with a difference of about 3°C between the warmer south and cooler north in January and a 1° difference in July. The oceanic influence is also more distinct in January.

One should not get the impression from the 4°–7°C January average that frosts or sub-zero air temperatures do not occur. These values are averages of the 24-hour day, and include low night-time as well as much higher mid-afternoon values.

The locally higher temperatures in the vicinities of Dublin and Cork are explained on page 120. The reader should also note that the data are expressed as "reduced to mean sea level". Hence the lower temperatures associated with increasing altitude are not represented. Neither could the contrast between south-facing and north-facing slopes be shown on a map of this scale.

Rohan, P.K., 1986. The Climate of Ireland. The Stationery Office, Dublin.

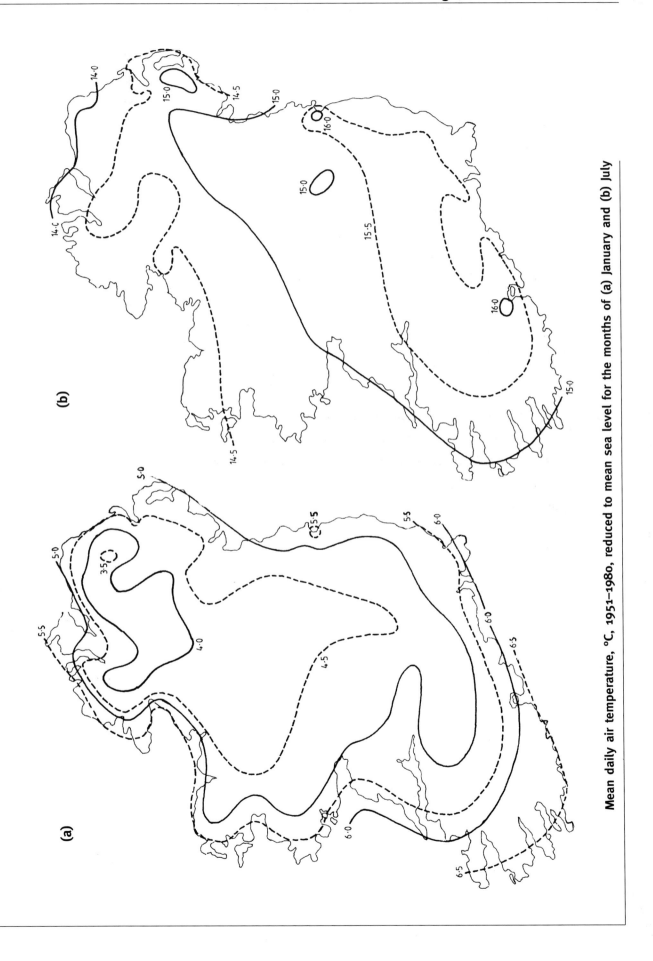

Mean daily air temperature, °C, 1951–1980, reduced to mean sea level for the months of (a) January and (b) July

January minimum and July maximum air temperatures

A comparison of how cold January nights are and how warm July days are gives a good approximation of the extremes of our air temperatures. The relatively small amount of solar radiation received during the short winter days is less than the long-wave outgoing radiation that occurs day and night and hence air temperatures fall. The lowest temperatures are recorded when outgoing radiation losses are augmented by cold easterly winds arriving from the Eurasian landmass. The pattern is not the same everywhere, and when averaged over a standard 30-year period, we can see a latitudinal as well as a coastal influence. The warm waters of the Atlantic do not cool as much as the more inland areas with the result that there is about a 3.5°C difference between the peninsulas of Munster and inland areas in Ulster. It should be noted that the values given are averages of some nights with values below zero and others with substantially higher values.

The pattern is reversed somewhat in July, with the difference in the respective heat capacities of land and water again evident. During the long summer days the land surfaces absorb heat more efficiently than water, and temperatures rise. The greater heat capacity of water and its continual mixing and movement do not allow the temperatures of coastal regions to rise as much as in the inland counties. The higher proportion of wet soils and open bodies of water in the northern half of the country augments the general latitudinal differences between Munster/Leinster and Ulster/Connaght. It is to be emphasised that all the data are given as if the land were all at sea level; elevated and north-sloping areas will tend to be cooler and south-facing slopes warmer.

Rohan, P.K., 1975. The Climate of Ireland. The Stationery Office, Dublin.

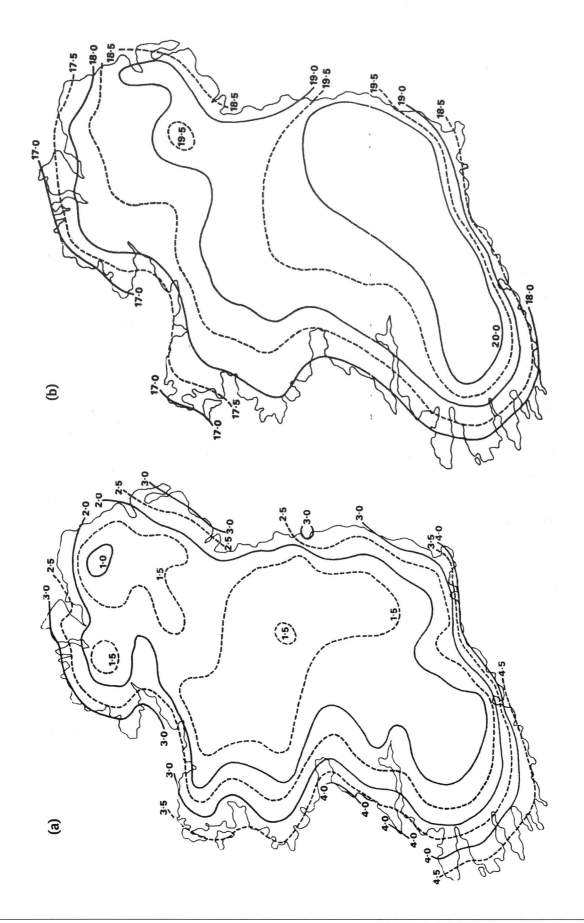

Air temperatures, °C, 1931–1960, reduced to mean sea level: (a) January mean daily minimum and (b) July mean daily maximum

Air frost

Air frost is recorded when the thermometers in the Stevenson screens read zero or minus values on the Celsius scale. This is a fairly common occurrence in winter nights, but its effect is of greater significance in autumn and spring when tender crops are exposed. The mean dates of occurrence of the last air frost in spring and the first air frost in autumn are of considerable interest to farmers, foresters and gardeners amongst others. The patterns of the first and last frosts are shown here, together with probability tables which reflect the wide year-to-year variation around the median dates given.

The coastal–inland and north–south patterns typical of mean air temperatures are clear. The coastal advantage (of later dates of first autumn frosts and earlier dates of last spring frosts) is usually confined to a strip about 10 km wide, but broader in the deeply-incised, windy west coast.

Some maps plot the mean dates with "return periods" expressed in years. For example, a 5-year return-period is equivalent to a probability of occurrence of 20% and 10-year return-period event has, by definition, a probability of 10% in any one year.

These maps are based on air temperatures reduced to sea level, and from stations situated in open flat country; hence they do not show that air frost is more likely in certain localities. The severest frosts occur in low-lying areas known as "frost hollows". In closed or sheltered valleys, the mean date of last air frost in spring may be several weeks later than in open country. The mechanism of frost formation in hollows is partly due to air draining from surrounding land, but the exact process is unknown.

Rohan, P.K., 1975. The Climate of Ireland. The Stationery Office, Dublin.
Keane, T., 1986. Meteorological Parameters in Ireland. Chapter 3 in: Climate, Weather and Irish Agriculture, edited by T. Keane. Agmet Group, Dublin.

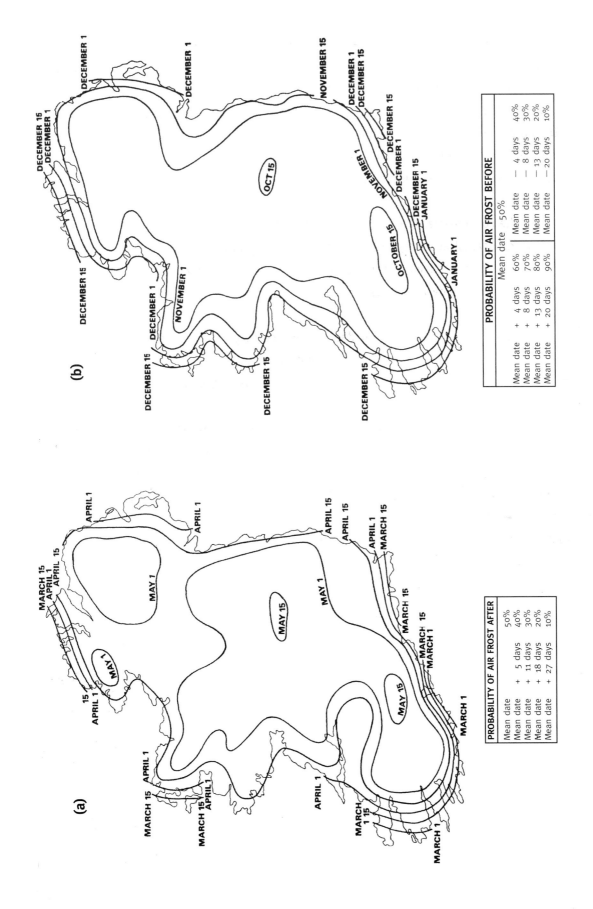

PROBABILITY OF AIR FROST BEFORE

	Mean date	50%	
Mean date	+ 4 days	60%	
Mean date	+ 8 days	70%	
Mean date	+ 13 days	80%	
Mean date	+ 20 days	90%	
Mean date	− 4 days	40%	
Mean date	− 8 days	30%	
Mean date	− 13 days	20%	
Mean date	− 20 days	10%	

PROBABILITY OF AIR FROST AFTER

Mean date		50%
Mean date	+ 5 days	40%
Mean date	+ 11 days	30%
Mean date	+ 18 days	20%
Mean date	+ 27 days	10%

Mean date of (a) last air frost in spring and (b) first air frost in autumn, 1944–1968, reduced to mean sea level

Soil and earth temperatures

The soil is a net receiver of solar radiation in the summer and a net emitter of long-wave radiation in the winter. Hence it has an annual cycle of temperature variation which may be plotted graphically for selected depths (which are usually 100, 200, 300, 600 and 1200 mm). This graph shows the long-term annual pattern of soil and earth temperature at Kilkenny synoptic station. The data show that the upper 100 mm has the greatest fluctuation—warmest in June, coldest in January. Since it takes the soil a while to warm up and to transmit heat downwards, the maximum temperature at greater depths is recorded a week or two later—the maximum at 1.2 m is not reached at Kilkenny on average until about August 1st—and at a lower value, 15°C, compared with 18°C at the surface in June. Likewise minimum soil temperatures are recorded at the surface in mid January and at increasingly later dates with depth. The temperature damping continues with increasing depth, so that at about 10 m depth there is little or no difference between winter and summer. Hence many animals can hibernate comfortably in burrows and caves, and water drawn from deep wells is always at the same temperature.

The pattern shown here is for a well-drained soil. Wetter soils will have flatter "peaks" and maximum and minimum temperatures will be recorded at later dates at all depths. The extreme is reached in blanket peats (which contain over 90% water when undrained). In these, the lag is so great (due to the low heat conductivity of immobile water) that the maximum surface temperatures are recorded in late summer and the maximum subsurface temperatures (at say 1.2 m) are not reached until December.

A similar pattern of soil temperature fluctuation occurs daily—coldest in the early morning, warmest in the early afternoon. It is most obvious in summer time, and has a similar lag pattern with depth (though the daily effect only reaches to a few mm). The nature of the vegetation, soil and land use will modify both the diurnal and annual patterns.

Keane, T., 1986. Meteorological Parameters in Ireland. Chapter 3 in: Climate, Weather and Irish Agriculture, edited by T. Keane. Agmet Group, Dublin.

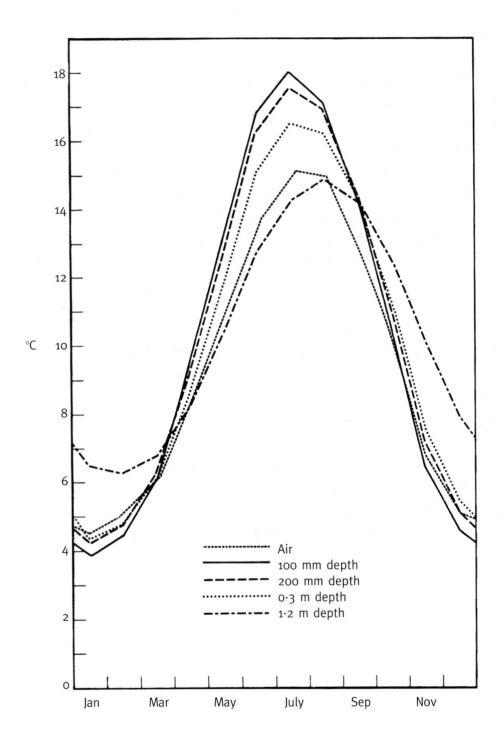

Monthly mean air, soil (100–300 mm depths) and earth (1.2 m depth) temperatures, °C, 1958–1982, throughout the year at Kilkenny

Urban climates

The air temperature maps (pages 111–115) show elevated mean and minimum temperatures in the vicinity of Dublin and Cork. This is a phenomenon of urban areas worldwide, and while it is not confined to temperature variation, the term 'heat island' is used for the climatic contrast between urban areas and the surrounding countryside.

The elevated temperatures arise from the thermal capacity and heat conductivity of building and paving materials, and to a lesser extent, the heat produced by industrial, commercial, domestic and transport activities in cities. Temperature differences between the city and the surrounding countryside are greatest by night and in the winter. Maximum, minimum and mean air temperatures for Co. Dublin (1951–1980) are mapped here. A difference of 1°C between the mean temperatures for the urban heat island and the surrounding countryside is about average for medium-to-large cities worldwide.

Associated with elevated temperatures are changes in other parameters: more cloud, fog and rain, and in some, more hail and thunderstorms; there is likely to be less frost and snow; lighter, though relatively more gusty winds and lower humidity, especially in summer. As a consequence city plants bud and bloom earlier, some birds find attractive urban habitats, and less space heating is required. Many of the advantages are counterbalanced by air pollution, especially smoke, haze and photochemical smog.

Anon., 1983. The Climate of Dublin. Meteorological Service, Dublin.
See also Graham, E., 1993. The urban heat island of Dublin city during the summer months. Irish Geography 26 (1): 45–57.

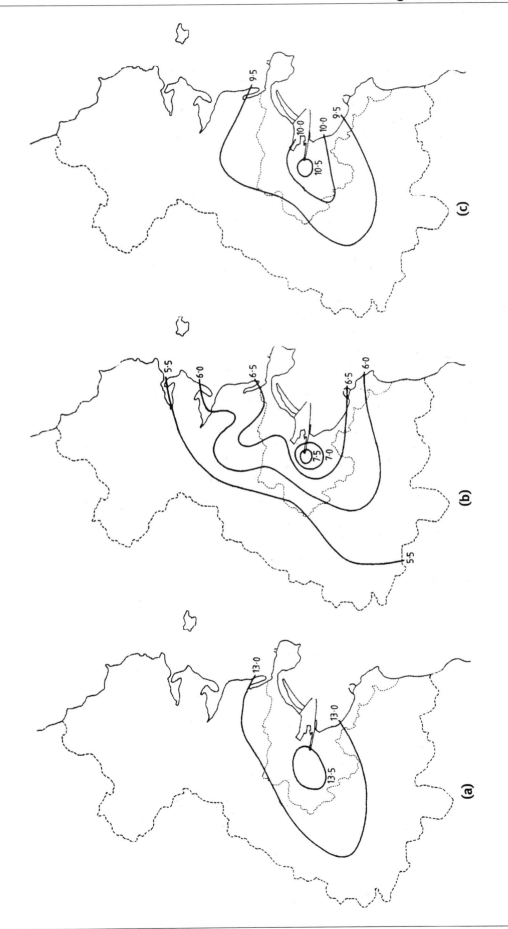

Air temperatures, °C, for Co. Dublin, near sea level, 1951–1980: (a) mean daily maximum air temperature; (b) mean daily minimum air temperature and (c) mean air temperature

Relative humidity

Visitors to this country from continental climates often comment on the dampness of the Irish climate, even though it may not be visibly wet. They claim that in summer they feel more clammy and that our "cold" winters are not reflected by the actual temperature data. What these visitors are experiencing is a climate where relative humidity seldom falls below 75% and is often 85–90%. This parameter of our climate is a measure of how much water vapour is in the air. Its correct definition is the proportion of water vapour actually present in the air at a given temperature relative to the maximum equilibrium amount that could be held in the air at that temperature. It can be measured in a number of ways, the chief instruments being (1) a hair hygrograph (which uses the variation in the length of a web of human hair with humidity) and (2) a psychrometer (which uses the differences in temperature between an ordinary thermometer and a similar one that is kept constantly wet on the outside—evaporation from the wet bulb lowers its temperature, and the rate of evaporation depends on the relative humidity).

Compared with other mapped parameters in this atlas, there is very little geographical or indeed temporal variation in relative humidity values in Ireland. In keeping with rainfall and other patterns, values are higher in January (map (a)) than in July (b). The annual mean value (map (c)) ranges from 75-80% for most of the island. There is a general decrease inland in the summer due to increasing temperature with distance from the sea.

Relative humidity is an important parameter from an agricultural and horticultural point of view. It is related to actual evapotranspiration and governs a number of growth factors, disease conditions and harvesting operations. Map (a) should be compared with the pattern of Effective Blight Hours (page 173), used to predict potato blight, and on which blight warnings are issued.

Goudie, A.S. and Brunsden, D., 1994. The Environment of the British Isles An Atlas. Oxford University Press, Oxford. Reproduced by permission of Oxford University Press.

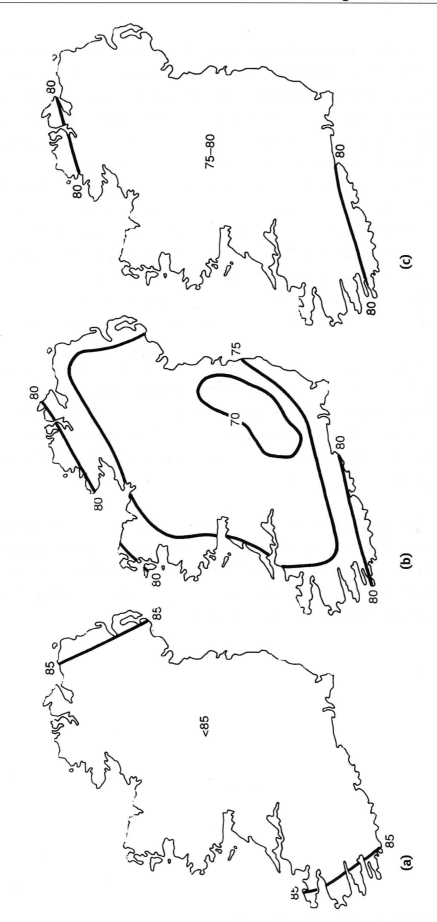

Mean relative humidity, %, for (a) January, (b) July and (c) the whole year

Global solar radiation, Ireland and Britain

Virtually all the energy we receive at the surface of the earth comes from the sun in the form of solar radiation. Less than half of the incoming radiation comes directly towards us because of the atmosphere around the earth; normally the total (or global) amount of radiation is made up of 40% direct radiation and 60% diffuse. In cloudy periods the radiation may be 100% diffuse (while the total will be considerably lower). The amount of solar radiation received is measured at some synoptic stations. The usual unit is MJ m^{-2} (megajoules per square metre). Because of the angle of inclination and the rotation of the earth, the amount received changes seasonally as well as daily.

The four small maps (a–d) show the average daily receipt of global solar radiation for a month in each season. The values for Ireland are about 9 MJ m^{-2} in March, 18–20 in June, 10–11 in September and 1.5–2 in December. The mean annual value is about 10 MJ m^{-2}. There is a slight latitudinal trend with monthly differences of about 1.5–2 MJ m^{-2} between the south coast and the northern counties. Despite a difference in latitude, the southeast of Ireland has very similar values to southwest England.

The radiation received can have any of several fates, including heating air, water or soil, evaporating water and—especially important—taking part in photosynthesis. A proportion of the energy is reflected, and the balance is re-radiated back to space as long-wave radiation. The short-term difference between incoming and outgoing radiation is net radiation. In the long term there is a balance between incoming and outgoing radiation. Since net radiation is a measure of the energy available at the earth's surface it is a more useful value than global (total) radiation, and so net radiation is now recorded at two Irish stations—Kilkenny and Valentia.

Collingbourne, R.H., 1976. Radiation and sunshine. Chapter 4 in: The Climate of the British Isles, edited by T.J. Chandler and S. Gregory. Longman, London.

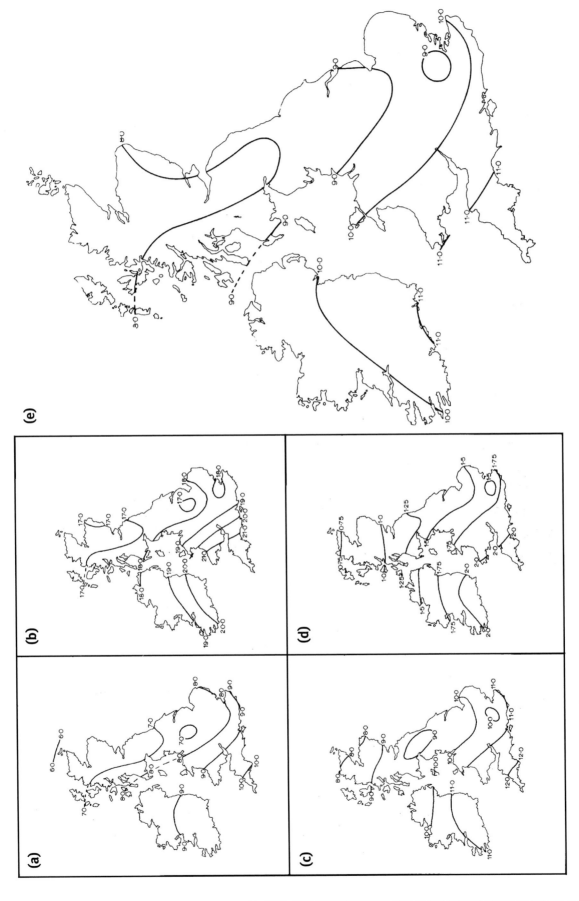

Average daily totals of global solar radiation, MJ/(m² day): (a) March; (b) June; (c) September; (d) December; (e) year

Bright sunshine

Before the measurement of radiation became possible the amount of energy reaching the earth's surface could be assessed by measuring the duration of bright sunshine. The equipment was (and is) based on a glass sphere which focuses sunlight on a special card, thereby causing it to burn or scorch. It is not a very accurate measurement when sunshine is interrupted by showers or when sunshine is unusually hot.

Map (a) depicts the annual total duration of bright sunshine in hours in Ireland. As with many parameters there is a coastal influence as well as a latitudinal trend. The claim to "the sunny southeast" is justified since there are more than 1600 hours of sunshine in the Rosslare area, while the coastal strip from Dublin to Cork experiences about 1500 hours per year. The rest of the country averages 1200 to 1400 hours. Lower values in the north midlands and in the mountainous regions (as little as 1100 hours in parts of Kerry) are due to the development of convective and orographic cloud, respectively.

Over the year as a whole the mean daily duration of bright sunshine is between 3.5 and 4 hours; along the south and east coasts the average exceeds 4 hours, peaking above 4.5 hours per day in the extreme southeast (map (b)).

Rohan has shown the month by month data in map form. The sunniest months are May and June, during which the duration averages between 5 and 6.5 hours per day over most of Ireland. Rosslare averages over seven hours per day during these months. In contrast, the averages for December and January are generally between one and two hours. The southeast–northwest trend is maintained throughout each month, with local variations for more hilly areas.

Rohan, P.K., 1986. The Climate of Ireland. The Stationery Office, Dublin.
Keane, T., 1988. Features of the Irish climate of importance to agriculture: comparison with neighbouring Europe, in: Proceedings of Conference on Weather and Agriculture, edited by T. Keane. Agmet Group, Dublin.

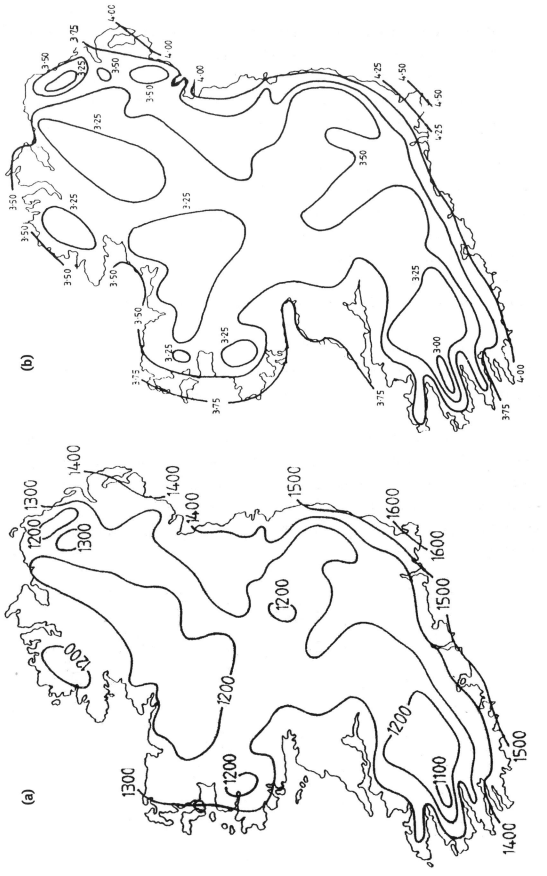

Duration of bright sunshine, 1951–1980: (a) Mean annual total duration of bright sunshine, h/year; (b) Mean daily duration of bright sunshine, h/day.

Wind

Our knowledge of wind speed and direction is based on anemometers and wind vanes installed in synoptic and climatological stations as well as on estimates made by experienced observers. The movement of air is generated by the unequal heating of the earth's surface and the formation of zones of high and low pressure. This pattern is modified by the rotation of the earth and by topographic barriers such as mountains and hills.

Map (a) shows the pattern of mean annual wind speed at 10 m above ground level. It is a fairly simple pattern with relatively light wind conditions inland and much stronger winds along the coasts. The higher values are recorded along the northwest coast due to the proximity to Atlantic depression tracks between Ireland and Iceland.

Map (b) plots the frequency of wind directions at the synoptic stations. The thicknesses of the lines indicate different wind strength classes from each direction. The most frequent winds are southwesterly, but this is modified by local conditions. For example, at Shannon airport, the most frequent winds follow the east–west line of the estuary, while Dublin is sheltered by the Wicklow mountains to the south.

These maps fail to show the much greater windspeeds on exposed promontories or mountain tops. The following examples show the difference between windspeeds at elevated sites and the appropriate meteorological station nearby.

Hill-top site	Altitude (m)	Windspeed (m s^{-1})	Met. Station Windspeed (m s^{-1})
Bloody Foreland	320	11.4	8.1
Slieve Gullion	583	11.2	4.4
Three Rock Mountain	461	6.4	5.2
Mount Gabriel	412	8.6	5.5

Rohan, P.K., 1975. The Climate of Ireland. The Stationery Office, Dublin.
Rohan, P.K., 1986. The Climate of Ireland. The Stationery Office, Dublin.

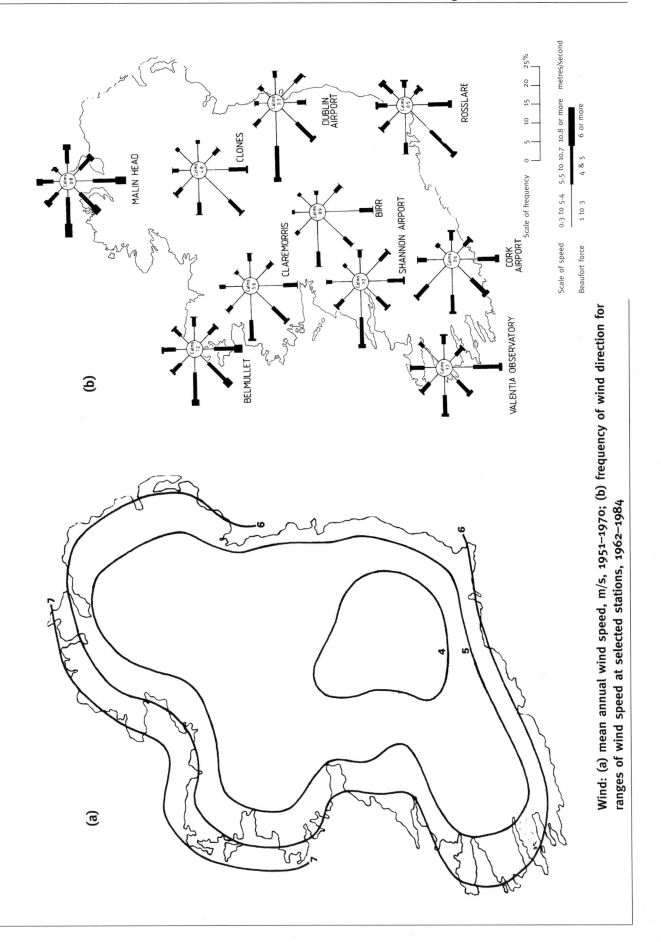

Wind: (a) mean annual wind speed, m/s, 1951–1970; (b) frequency of wind direction for ranges of wind speed at selected stations, 1962–1984

Daily pattern of wind speed

Just as the unequal heating of the earth's surface sets up major global pressure zones, the fact that the ground surface heats up by day and cools at night is responsible for much of the hour-to-hour variation in wind speed measured at synoptic stations. Hence, regardless of the overall values for wind speed, the greatest speed, averaged over a period of 20–30 years, occurs between 12 noon and 3 pm, and the least between 2 am and 6 am. The actual range of wind speeds during any particular day may be very much larger than shown here. However, since the arrival of gales and storms happens at random throughout the 24 hours of the diurnal cycle, their variation is not obvious in long-term hourly means.

Since there is more radiation available for heating the ground surface in summer, the largest difference between the lowest and highest velocities is recorded in the summer months. Graph (b) compares the January and July values at Clones and Belmullet. January records the higher mean speeds, but the difference between early morning and early afternoon is much more distinct, using mean values, in July. Similar differences exist between cloudy and sunny days.

Advantage can be taken of these fairly subtle differences. A farmer wishing to dry hay, or a housekeeper to dry clothes will do best to work mid-morning in advance of the best drying conditions in the afternoon. People spraying pesticides where spray drift is to be avoided can make good use of the calmer periods early and late in the day. In fact contractors in other countries who have large acreages to spray may work all night to minimise the chances of spray drift.

Rohan, P.K., 1975. The Climate of Ireland. The Stationery Office, Dublin.
Rohan, P.K., 1986. The Climate of Ireland. The Stationery Office, Dublin.

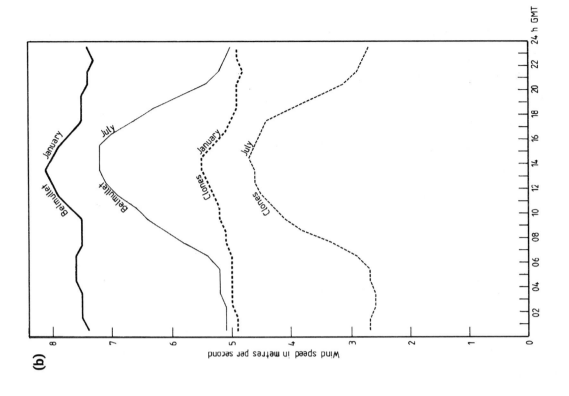

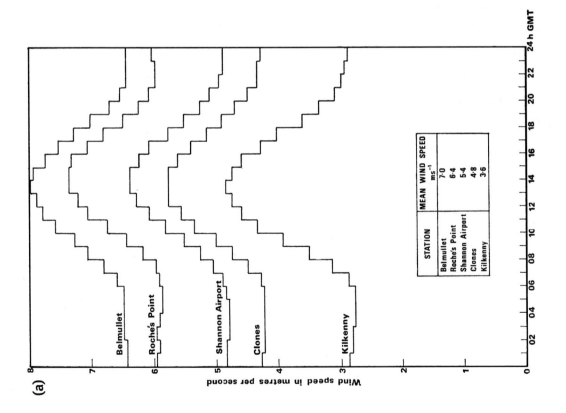

Mean wind speed, m/s, between exact hours at selected stations: (a) annual mean, 1961–1970; (b) January and July means, 1962–1984

Driving rain is a term that describes the combined effects of falling rain and strong winds. Most rain falls vertically in calm conditions, but when a strong wind blows, rain drops are carried more horizontally. A vertical or inclined surface in the path of driven rain will receive much more rain than under light wind conditions.

This is a map of driving rain index, which is the product of mean annual wind-speed (m/s, see page 128) and mean annual rainfall (m/year, see page 98). Since wind direction is not taken into account, the index serves only as a rough guide. However, it is a useful parameter both to the farming and non-farming public. Apart from discomfort and even danger on exposed hillsides, driving rain gets into places which vertically-falling rain does not. It penetrates into unprotected haystacks, bales, sheds and temporary shelters, disturbs the insulation in sheep fleeces, causes widespread lodging of cereals and transfers disease organisms by splashing.

The map shows a west-to-east as well as an altitudinal trend. All the mountainous areas have values of 10 to 15 m^2/(s year), while the lowlands, especially in the east central areas have a driving rain index below 5. The worst rain penetration occurs in a relatively few but rather prolonged rainfall events, and near the south and east coasts a slow-moving depression can occasionally give a lengthy spell of persistent rain driven by winds between north and east in direction.

A map such as this may help to explain why, in former times, home owners in the west of Ireland were very reluctant to extend their houses on the western side. Prior to the availability of good flashing materials for sealing the joints, it was difficult to prevent the driven rain from penetrating between the old and new.

Rohan, P.K., 1986. The Climate of Ireland. The Stationery Office, Dublin.

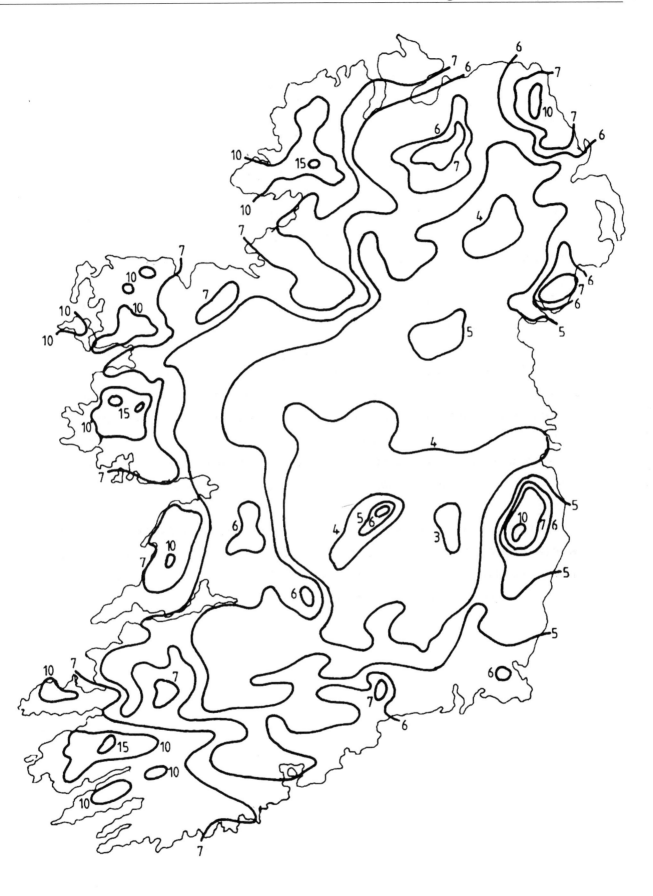

Driving rain index, m²/(s year)

Potential evapotranspiration

Water is essential for the growth of plants and much of the annual fall of rain is used up by growing plants. This water is taken in by the rootlets and root hairs and is transferred through the roots and stems of plants to the leaves. Here it undergoes a change to the vapour state and is evaporated from the leaf surface into the atmosphere. This is transpiration. Whenever plant surfaces are wet, that surface water also evaporates. The combined process is known as evapotranspiration. Since plants vary in size (tree, grass, moss), shape, age, life cycle and so on, the amount of water used by them varies enormously. Likewise, climate has a major role in how much water can be evaporated from leaf surfaces and critical parameters in this process are temperature, relative humidity and wind.

The amount of water actually evaporated in any one year at any one place varies considerably, due to weather conditions, and the availability of water. In dry spells, there may be a lot of "drying", but nothing to dry—evaporation from soil and leaf surfaces is far short of that which is possible. Potential evapotranspiration is standardised as the evaporation occuring from a short grass sward supplied with adequate water and nutrients, and is measured in the same units as precipitation.

Map (a) shows the pattern of average annual potential evapotranspiration from the cold north to the warm south of Europe and gives an average value of 500 mm for Ireland. Britain ranges from ‹400 mm to ›600 mm, while as much as 1300 mm of water could be evaporated in southern Europe if it were available. Map (b) shows Britain and Ireland in greater detail with coastal Ireland having a value of about 500 mm and inland areas 450 mm or less.

Ward, R.C., 1976. Evaporation, Humidity and the Water Balance. Chapter 7 in: The Climate of the British Isles, edited by T.J. Chandler and S. Gregory. Longman, London.

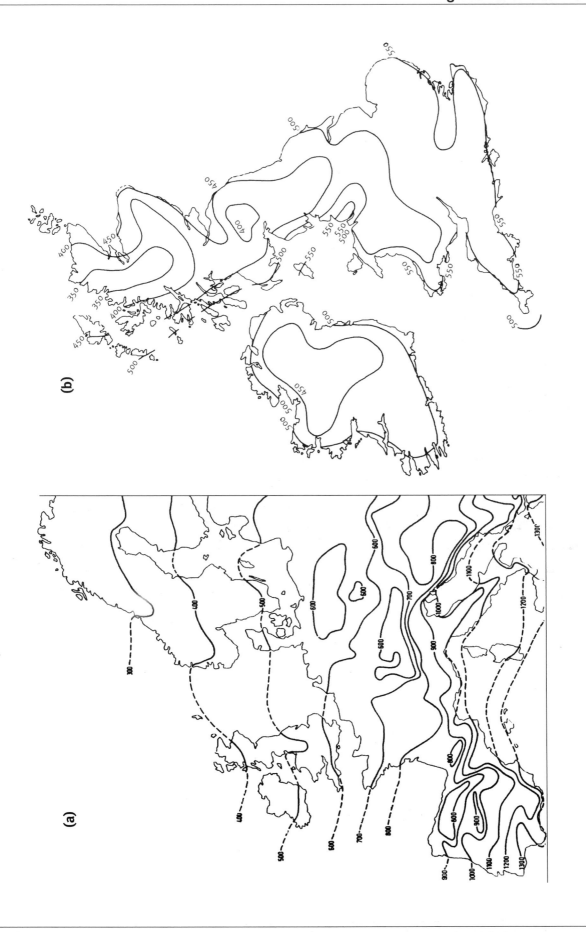

Mean annual potential evapotranspiration, mm/year: (a) Europe; (b) Britain and Ireland

Winter and summer potential evapotranspiration

Because of our climate, most plants and crops grow in the April–September period. Hence the amount of water available for transpiration and that actually transpired by plants govern, to a large extent, the annual yield of many crops. However, the amount of water removed from crop and soil surfaces in the October–March period is also critical to many farm operations. For example, trafficability and workability of soils depend on the amount of water they contain both in autumn and in early spring.

The amount of water which can be transpired by plants and evaporated to the air in winter and summer is shown in these maps. Both have a strong coastal–inland trend, especially in the winter months where the aerodynamic part of the process is favoured by the greater windiness of the coastal areas. By adding the values for both periods a slight latitudinal pattern emerges, reflecting the greater radiation receipts of the south coast. Here the annual value is given as 575 mm on the west-Munster peninsulas, while the value for the cooler inland northwestern counties approximates 450 mm.

Monthly values of potential evapotranspiration are measured at a number of synoptic and climatological stations. The Meteorological Service also publishes ten-day values for potential evapotranspiration. Values for shorter periods are usually unreliable.

Meteorological Service, Dublin.

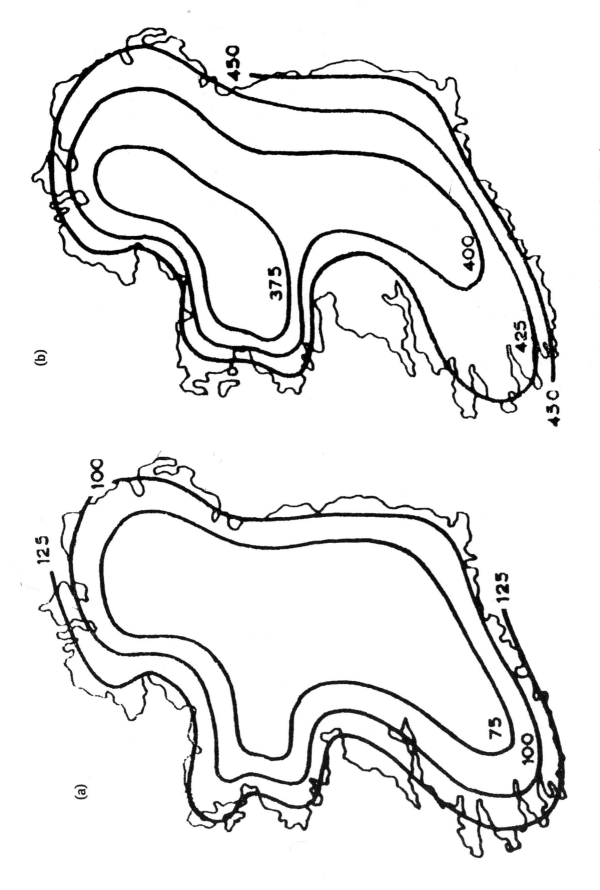

Mean potential evapotranspiration, mm, during 1958–1972 for the six-month periods (a) winter, October–March and (b) summer, April–September

Water deficits mean different things to different people. Water is an essential requirement for a whole range of enterprises and even temporary shortages can cause problems and losses. The two groups who are most concerned about deficits are those who grow crops and those who must provide a reliable supply of water for municipal, industrial and domestic uses. Farmers, horticulturists and agronomists are amongst the first, while hydrologists, engineers and public utility managers are amongst the second.

While meteorologists calculate that a potential water deficit exists when rainfall is less than potential evapotranspiration rates, hydrologists put emphasis on the level of surface water and groundwater resources. The most likely time for soil-moisture and groundwater reserves to show significant deficit is in the late summer or early autumn.

Map (a) shows the mean distribution of accumulated potential water deficits at the end of the four months of most active growth, May–August. It has a distinct south-east–northwest trend in line with patterns of rainfall, temperature, sunshine duration and potential evaporation values. It is a meteorologic parameter, which does not take into account catchment properties, permeability, crops or soils.

The potential water deficits accumulated for the entire year can be used to esti-mate whether there are likely to be "windows of opportunity", during which farmers can carry out on-farm operations successfully. These include late-season harvesting, autumn/winter sowing and application of slurry or fertilizers.

Map (b) shows the country placed in four regions on the basis of assumed cumu-lative soil moisture deficits calculated on 12-month rainfall and evapotranspiration data. Coupled with information on individual or local soils, better managerial judgements can be made which are beneficial both economically and environmentally.

Rohan, P.K., 1986. The Climate of Ireland. The Stationery Office, Dublin.
Gardiner, M.J., 1986. Use of soil and climatic data to predict hydraulic loading behaviour of Irish soils. Soil Use and Management 2 (4): 146–149.

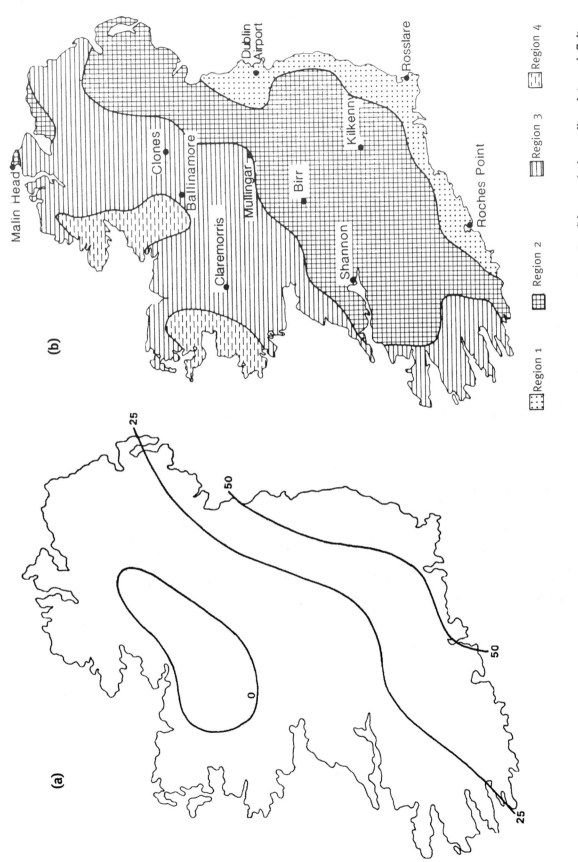

Water deficits: (a) mean accumulated potential water deficit, mm, May to August, 1958–1965; **(b)** cumulative soil moisture deficit regions. The values given for the different regions are: Region 1, 105·3; Region 2, 57·7; Region 3, 20; Region 4, 2 mm.

This map shows areas which had different temperature conditions on a single night and day, due to the weather conditions prevailing, and their interaction with topography, as seen from infrared satellite imagery. The weather at the time was exceptionally cold, with nighttime air temperatures down to -12°C, and daytime maxima in many areas no higher than -3°C. The regions observed may be summarised as follows:

Coastal belts governed by sea temperature; inland penetration of warm air is stopped by high ground, but can go far inland where topography allows: units 1, 4, 10, 14, 16, 20, 23, 28, 29, 30, 32 and 33. Unit 16 is interrupted by cold air draining from the Boyne and Liffey valleys.

Cold basins defined by surrounding high ground on two, three or four sides, in some cases open to the sea but not strongly influenced by it: units 3, 5, 6, 8, 11, 12, 13, 22, 24, 25, 27 and 31. Unit 31 encloses a warm core of Lough Neagh.

Cold cores of high ground with cold air draining off high ground onto lower areas, modified by extensive forest cover where present: units 2, 9, 15, 21 and 26.

Thermal plateaux of rather constant temperatures, with warmer areas of low ground near lakes: units 7, 17, 18 and 19. Unit 17 encloses cold valleys, of which the Boyne Valley is a good example.

The thermal regions defined here apply only to a single 24-hour period of exceptional cold, where the temperature regimes were dominated by radiative cooling and heating, the thermal properties of the land surface, topographic controlling of gentle air movement, and drainage of cold air from high ground to low. Very different regions may be definable under other weather conditions, but this approach opens up new ways of defining regional and local climates.

Tyrrell, J.G., 1983. Meteosat 2 imagery and the distribution of low surface temperatures in Ireland. Irish Geography 16: 79–94.

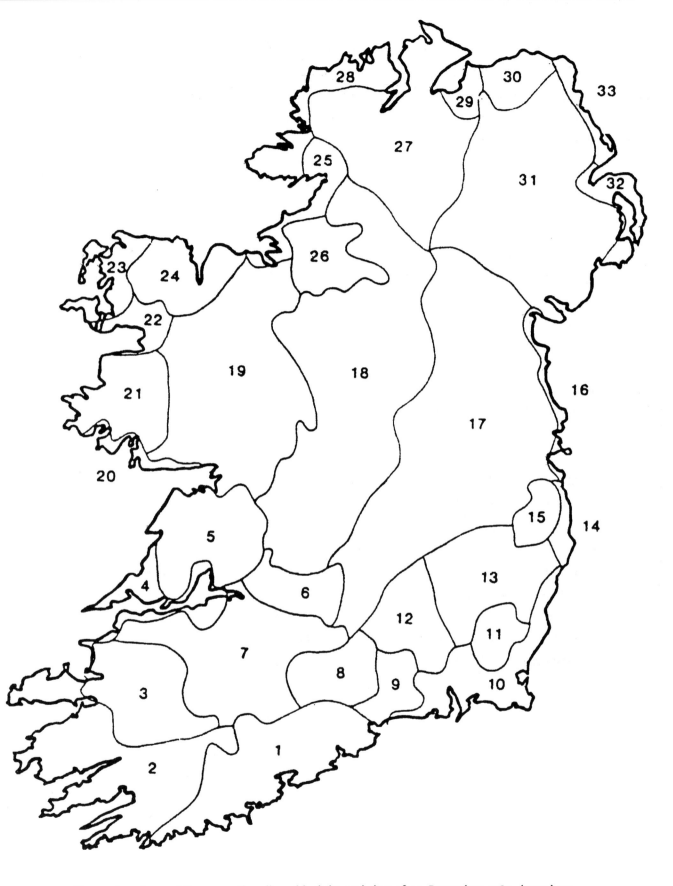

Thermal regions of the exceptionally cold night and day of 12–December 1982, based on infrared imagery from the Meteosat 2 satellite

Chemical climate

Since water is a powerful solvent there is no pure water in nature. A wide range of substances which are present in the atmosphere become dissolved in the rain. Irish rain, most of it coming from the Atlantic, is especially rich in anions and cations associated with marine conditions. Chief among these are the cations of sodium, magnesium, calcium, potassium and the anions of chlorine and sulphur. The amount received varies with the element but increases with altitude, proximity to the Atlantic, and with the structure and surface area of the vegetation. In addition to the marine ions and those from other natural sources, there are significant quantities of ions and compounds in the atmosphere and in precipitation arising from municipal, industrial and agricultural sources. The most studied of these in recent years have been the ions sulphate, nitrate and ammonium, as well as the gases sulphur dioxide, ozone, nitrogen oxides, hydrocarbons and chlorofluorocarbons.

This map gives estimated mean annual deposition of total acidity, as moles of charge per hectare-year, mol/(ha year), based on precipitation analysis (from stations on page 83) for various periods, mostly in the mid 1980s, precipitation values (as mapped on page 101) for 1951–1980, and altitude. Total acidity for this purpose is taken as the sum of non-marine sulphate, nitrate and ammonium, less the sum of base cations.

Aherne, J.J. (private communication, 1995). Forest Ecosystem Research Group. University College, Dublin.

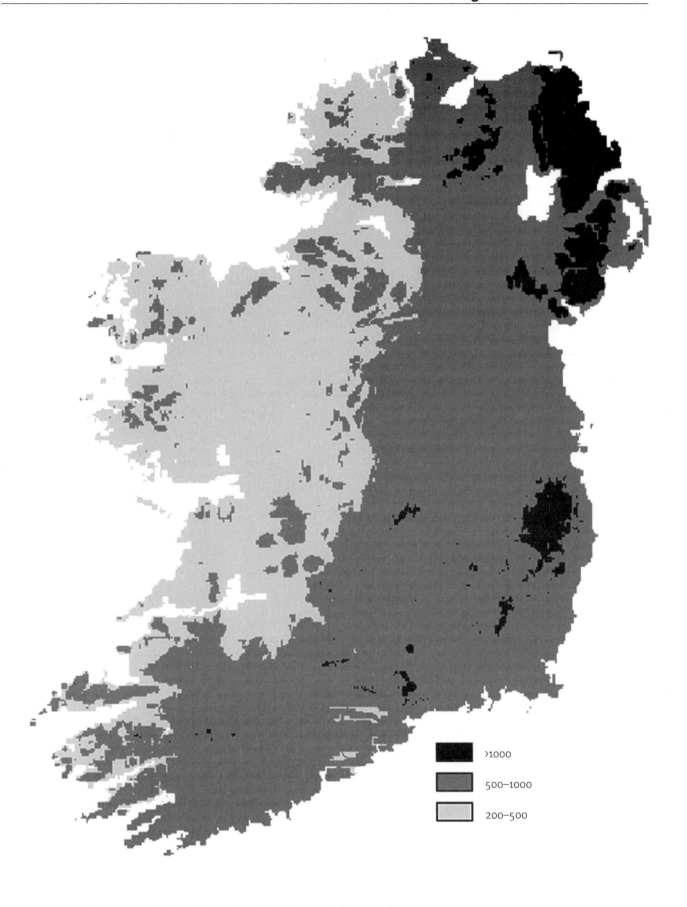

⬛	>1000
▨	500–1000
▨	200–500

Mean annual deposition of total acidity, mol /(ha year)

A note on small scale maps

The maps presented in the first sections of this atlas contain factual data in a visual form extracted from a variety of sources. In most instances they are generalised maps. That is, unlike reconnaissance maps (which are usually published at similarly small scales) the information they portray is simplified and reduced from a larger and more complex bank of data (whether in map, tabular, digital or other form), in order to make it more easily understood, and avoid clutter on the page. They are designed to depict a broad view and are particularly designed for educational use. They are not intended as technical documents to be used in planning, legal, administrative or other critical situations without a full aquaintance with their limitations.

While it could be said that all maps are generalisations of reality, a generalised map in the strict sense needs as much care in its construction as the original larger-scale and more precise map. A number of approaches are available, of which the most common approaches to generalisation are known as categoric, cartographic and spatial. Categoric generalisation finds its best expression in land-based maps such as geology, aquifer, soil or land-use maps. Here the boundaries between neighbouring parcels that are taxonomically similar are removed giving a map with fewer, but larger parcels and more broadly defined classes in the legend. For example, the soil series map of part of Co. Laois (page 47) shows a large number of mapping units, which are greatly reduced when presented for the whole island (page 41). Spatial generalisation is a form of cate-goric generalisation where dissimilar neighbours are amalgamated due to their consistent occurrence in observed positions. Grouping dissimilar soils which occur in a characteristic arrangement of a drumlin landscape into one mapping unit is a common example.

Climate elements lend themselves more easily to cartographic generalisation. In this operation the cartographer smooths intricate loops and undulations in the bound-aries, omits small "islands" and "peninsulas", joins delineations into larger ones and in general gives a simpler, combined pattern to the arrangement. In doing so a certain amount of information is lost, but done properly, the "errors" created should not detract from the usefulness of the map. Most of the isoline maps—such as rainfall, raindays, temperature, windspeed—have this type of generalisation.

The maps in the following section are based on the earlier maps and so are also generalised maps of small and very small scale. While some of them (such as the arable land and agricultural land maps) are derivative maps, most of the remainder are interpretative maps. Derivative maps are single-purpose or single-unit maps made for a specific purpose and do not add any new information for the user. Interpretative maps, especially the quality, capability or soil suitability maps, are based on categoric generalisation and incorporate additional information from other data banks. They can be loosely described as land use maps and as such incorporate the results of research and observation, collected locally or extracted from published sources. Most of these interpretative maps are focussed on the agricultural use of data, for example stocking rates or grazing season, while others are more strictly environmentally oriented, such as the aquifer vulnerability, run-off risk or critical load maps.

The user of these maps should be familiar with the original maps and of the role of the institutions and authors that made them in the first instance. They are very useful for acquiring a broad regional picture, but where site-specific data are required (as in environmental impact assessment), the pattern or rating suggested should be confirmed from the original data banks held by the Meteorological Service, Geological Survey, Teagasc or others, or by local investigation.

Land resources

The Land Resources map is based on the soil associations map and the five items in the legend are groups of similar soil associations. Lowland mineral (dry) is a combination of brown podzolic, grey-brown podzolic and brown earth soils (or associations dominated by these soils). Moderately wet mineral lowland is based on associations of poorly permeable soils, the parent materials of which include moulded tills (mostly as drumlin topography), marine tills and fine-textured shales and sandstones. "Lowland mineral (impermeable)" finds its greatest expression in the areas derived from Namurian shales, especially the Castlecomer, Abbeyfeale and Clare plateaux. The western drumlins are also in this category. Low level peat (blanket and/or raised) is extensive in the midland and mid-western lowlands and in Iar–Connacht/Erris. Mountain and hill land 'resources' range from sea level to the highest peaks, and from bare rock to deep peats.

From these descriptions it is clear that the capacity of soils for infiltration, percolation and disposal of water, beyond the amount necessary for production purposes, is fundamental to their use and suitablilty for agriculture.

An Foras Talúntais, Dublin.
Gardiner, M.J. and Radford, T., 1980. Soil Associations of Ireland and Their Land Use Potential. Soil Survey Bulletin No. 36. An Foras Talúntais, Dublin.

Mainly mountain and hill

Mainly low level peat

Mainly wet mineral

Land resources

Land quality—Northern Ireland

Land quality manifests itself as a combination of the attributes of the soil and those of the environment, especially climate. A classification of land for agricultural purposes takes into account the requirements of the crops and animals, the system of management and the local climate. The ability of soil to dispose of excess water and at the same time have enough water for transpiration in the summer is an important criterion. Hence, soils in elevated regions or in lowland depressions never make the top of the list.

This classification of land quality in Northern Ireland was based largely on the physical characteristics of the land. Its location or access was disregarded and the availability of artificial fertilizers meant that inherent chemical fertility was not of prime consideration. The legend shows that many of the unalterable soil characteristics such as texture, slope and depth were key criteria for placing land in the various categories.

This classification of suitability for agriculture is a single-purpose technical classification, and while useful for the purpose intended, does not allow for other uses; for example new crops, different management methods or non-agricultural uses.

Cruickshank, J.G., 1982. Soil. Chapter 8 in: Northern Ireland Environment and Natural Resources, edited by J.G. Cruickshank and D.N. Wilcock. The Queen's University Belfast and The New University of Ulster.

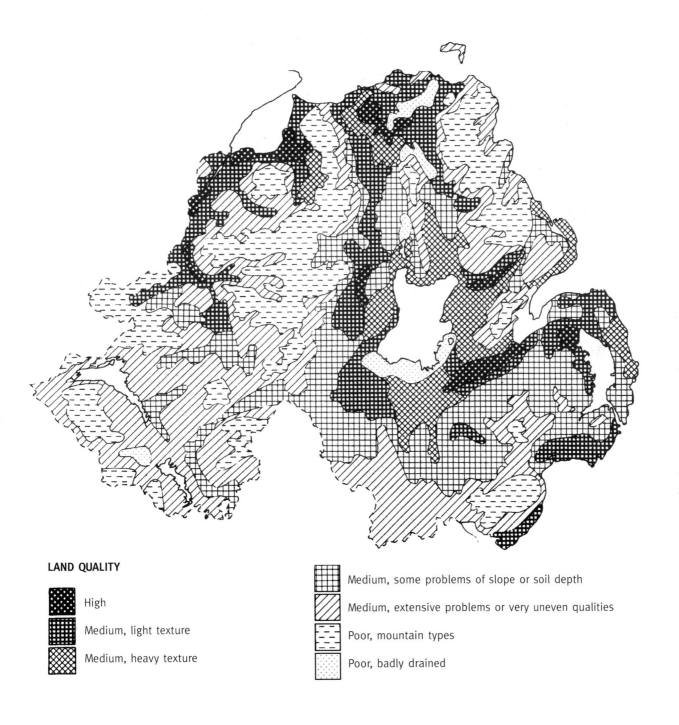

LAND QUALITY

High

Medium, light texture

Medium, heavy texture

Medium, some problems of slope or soil depth

Medium, extensive problems or very uneven qualities

Poor, mountain types

Poor, badly drained

Land Quality—Northern Ireland

Agricultural land

It is almost impossible to define "agricultural land" to the satisfaction of more than a few. At one extreme, there is overlap with horticulture, urbanisation and specialist uses, and at the other, land gradually changes into bare rock, flooded marshes, and non-agricultural crops such as conifer forest.

As a base for collecting census data, the Central Statistics Office regards agricultural land as the total area used for tillage crops, pasture and rough grazing. Regardless of soil type or agricultural enterprise more than half of Leinster and southeast Ulster are shown to have 85–100% of their area classed as agricultural land. Also in this category is all of Co. Limerick, south Co. Cork and parts of most Munster, Leinster and Ulster counties. The rest of the country is shown in descending rank in steps of 15%; only the steep mountain slopes of south Kerry and the blanket bog landscapes of Connemara, west Mayo and west Donegal are the lowest rank, with only 10–25% of their area being classed as "agricultural land".

Many parallels can be seen between the pattern of distribution of agricultural land and other maps, including physical features, soils, rainfall, wet-days, growing season, grazing season and many parameters of the agroclimatic environment.

Gillmor, D., 1989. Land, Work and Recreation. Chapter 6 in: The Irish Countryside, edited by D. Gillmor. Wolfhound Press, Dublin.

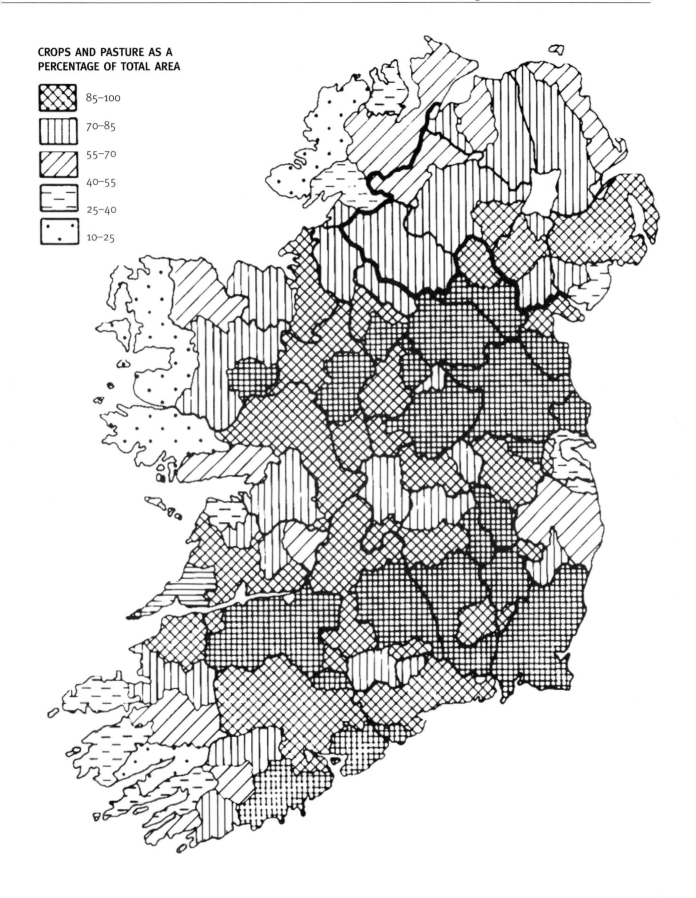

CROPS AND PASTURE AS A
PERCENTAGE OF TOTAL AREA

85–100

70–85

55–70

40–55

25–40

10–25

Improved agricultural land as a percentage of total area, by district electoral division

Non-arable land

Approximately 50% of the land of Ireland is suitable for cultivated cropping, leaving the remaining 50% more suited to other uses, both agricultural and non-agricultural. This map shows the general extent of both, as well as a classification of the non-arable land into three kinds—mountain/hill land, blanket and basin peat, and wet mineral lowland.

Reference to the Land Resources map (page 147) shows that the arable land has mostly dry and moderately-wet lowland mineral soils, while reference to Plate 6 shows that the principal soils which are arable belong to the luvisol, cambisol and some podzol and gleysol great groups. Non-arable land is generally based on podzols, gleysols, rendzinas, lithosols and histosols.

The reasons for this pattern of land capability are mostly related to climate. Other maps show that the north west has a much greater amount of precipitation, more rain-days, lower temperatures, less radiation and sunshine and differences in other parameters compared with the southeast and the south coast. These impinge on tillage farming in ways varying from opportunities to plough and cultivate, conditions conducive to germination and emergence, susceptibility to pests and diseases right through to ripening and harvesting. Hence the arable land outside the areas of the most versatile soils and the most amenable climates is devoted to the more undemanding pasture-grass crop. Even though in some years yields of cereals in many Irish counties surpass those of many parts of Europe, Irish farmers have found that grass-based farming is more dependable and profitable.

Culleton, E.B. and Gardiner, M.J., 1985. Economic Aspects of the Quaternary. Chapter 13 in: The Quaternary History of Ireland, edited by K.J. Edwards and W.P. Warren. Academic Press, London.

Mountain and Hill Land

Peatland { Blanket
          Basin

Wet Mineral Lowland

Non-arable land

Grass growing season

The ability of Irish land to grow grass is unquestioned. It is our most important crop, covering about 6.36 million hectares. While yields of 10–12 tonne/hectare of dry matter are high by international standards, 15–17.5 t/ha have been recorded under favourable conditions of climate and management. Very little growth takes place below an air temperature of 5°C, but there is a dramatic increase with increasing temperature to 10 or 12°C, above which growth continues to increase with increasing radiation, peaking at about 600 Watts per square metre. In addition to temperature and radiation, an adequate but not excessive amount of soil water is important, as is the maintenance of soil fertility.

These maps show the net effects of climate on active grass growth. All three show a southwest–northeast trend. Map (a) shows that grass begins to grow about the start of February in the coastal peninsulas of Cork and Kerry, where the influence of the sea temperatures on soil temperatures is greatest. With increasing distance inland or northwards, the beginning date becomes progressively later, and it may be the first of April in some years before grass actively springs to life in the high ground of central Ulster. The pattern is similar but reversed for the dates when active growth ceases in autumn, with a similar 6–8 week difference between the central Ulster counties and the southwestern peninsulas (map (b)).

Combining these data (map (c)) it can be seen that on average grass grows for the equivalent of eleven months in the coastal tips of Counties Cork and Kerry (330 days) and the growing season becomes progressively shorter with distance northeastwards. In the country around Lough Neagh, farmers can rely on an average of only eight months' active grass growth (240 days).

154

Connaughton, M.J., 1973. The Grass Growing Season in Ireland. Agrometeorological Merorandum No. 5. Irish Meteorological Service, Dublin.
Barry, P., 1986. Potential of Irish Climate for Agriculture. Chapter 13 in: Climate, Weather and Irish Agriculture, edited by T. Keane. Agmet Group, Dublin.

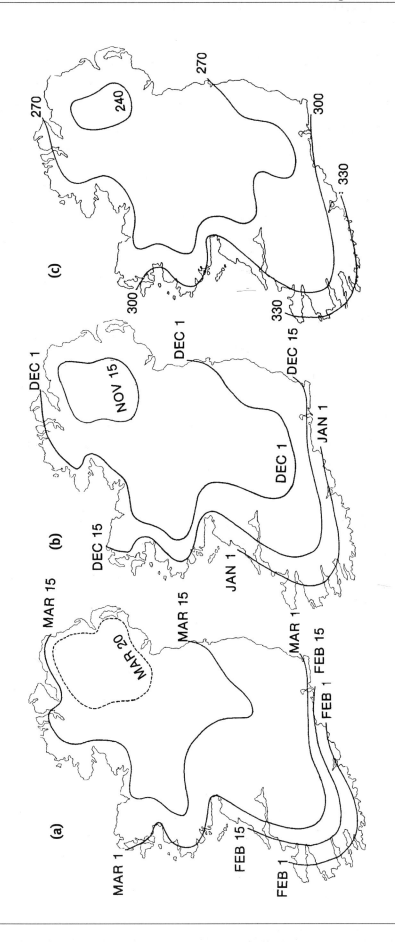

Grass growing season: (a) median dates of beginning; (b) median dates of ending, and (c) median length, days/year

Grass growing season in Northern Ireland

Map (c) on the previous page showed the estimated median length of the grass growing season in Northern Ireland to range from about 240 to almost 290 days, based mainly on temperatures reduced to sea level (as is the normal practice). These maps give the area in greater detail, and show the altitudinal effect on grass growth in Northern Ireland. The lapse in air temperature is about -0.7°C for each 100 m rise in altitude. The corresponding change in soil temperature at 30 cm is about -0.6°C, and the equivalent decrease in daily sunshine with altitude is about -0.2 hours.

As expected, the areas of shortest growing season are on the high hills and mountains (Antrim plateau, Mourne mountains, Sperrin mountains) where the number of days of significant grass growth varies in the range 220–235 per year. In the lowlands around Lough Neagh the value is 250–265. There is also a definite coastal effect especially obvious in the Ards peninsula and in the Lough Foyle region.

This set of maps also shows changing conditions between the 1940s and 1960s, the 1960–'70 decade having the shortest season and the least influence of sea temperatures.

Betts, N.L., 1982. Climate. Chapter 1 in: Northern Ireland Environment and Natural Resources, edited by J.G. Cruickshank and D.N. Wilcock. The Queen's University of Belfast and The New University of Ulster.

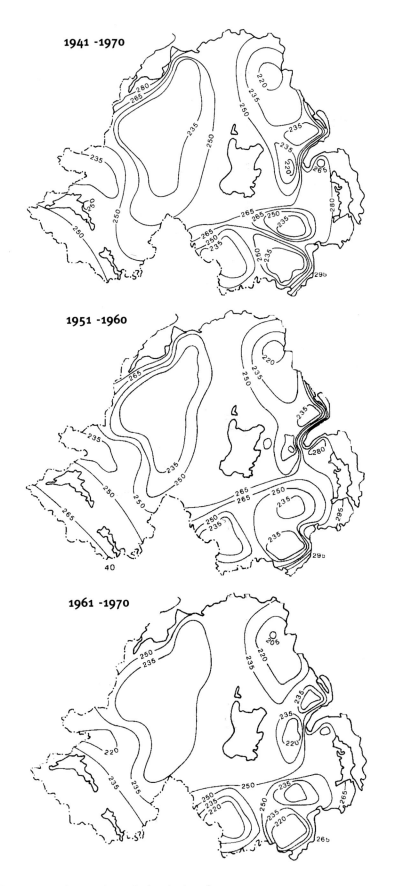

1941 -1970

1951 -1960

1961 -1970

Grass growing season in Northern Ireland, days/year

Accumulated temperatures and T-sum 200 dates

Accumulated temperatures, also known as degree days or thermal time, are useful indicators of progress in growth and development stages of crops. Normally, accumulated temperature is arrived at by choosing a date and a base temperature value suitable to a single crop or to a selection of crops. Since pasture grasses are by far the most extensively-grown crop in this country, conditions for their growth are the most commonly used parameters. A start-date of February 1st is usually used and degree-days above 5.6°C after that date are counted. Map (a) explains the suitability of land near the south coast for early grass growth. Degree days may be accumulated from January to December, May to October, or whatever is relevant to the crop in question. Other threshold temperatures such as 0°C and 10°C have also been used.

The term "T-sum 200 date" refers to the date at which a particular place will have experienced an accumulated temperature value of 200 degree-days over 5°C from a starting date of January 1st. This summation, which had its origins in the Netherlands, reflects the amount of heat absorbed and hence the amount of energy available to promote grass growth. It is used by farmers as an indication of conditions suitable for nitrogen application to grass swards. Map (b) shows that, averaged over the 20-year period 1961–1980, parts of Counties Cork and Kerry have accumulated enough heat by January 31st to make the application of fertilizer nitrogen a reasonable prospect (ie. that the nitrogen would be used by plants and not be leached or lost to runoff). Further north, it is wise to wait up to three weeks longer before applying nitrogen fertilizers.

Keane, T., 1988. Features of the Irish climate of importance to agriculture: comparison with neighbouring Europe. Proceedings of Conference on Weather and Climate, edited by T. Keane. Agmet Group, Dublin.

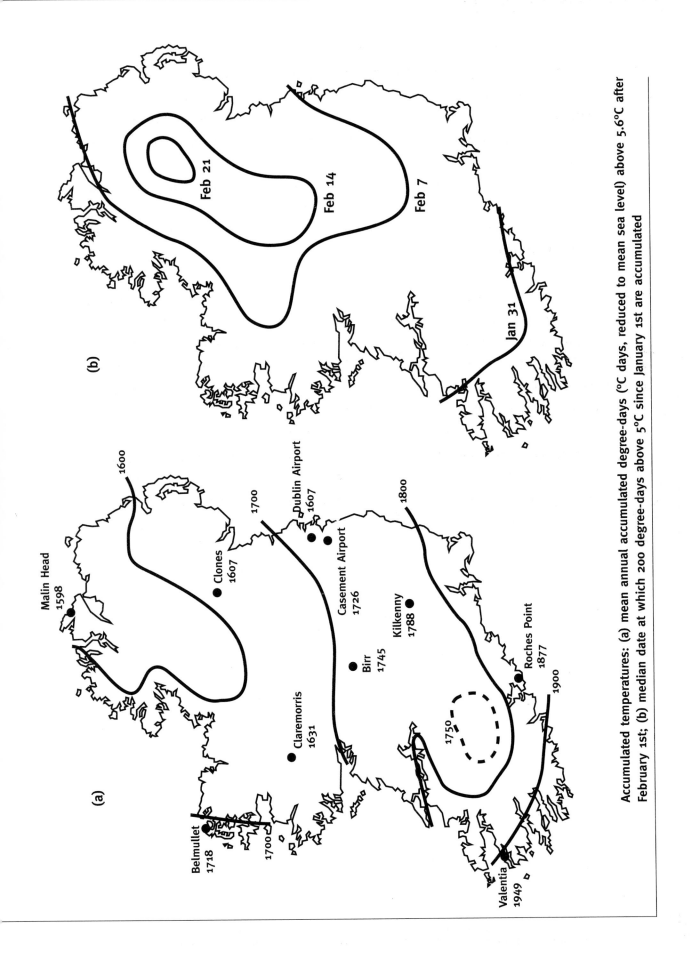

Accumulated temperatures: (a) mean annual accumulated degree-days (°C days, reduced to mean sea level) above 5.6°C after February 1st; (b) median date at which 200 degree-days above 5°C since January 1st are accumulated

Grazing season

Grazing season differs from grass-growing season in that animals and machines must be able to pass over the land surface without doing the soil and the crop any serious damage. It is frustrating to many farmers in spring to have plenty of grass for the animals but ground conditions unsuitable for traffic, especially by heavy animals. Hence a "correct" combination of soil moisture and soil temperature is the ideal for grass utilisation.

An attempt to combine soil trafficability with grass growth, the former being more dependent on the local rainfall and the latter being influenced mostly by temperature, is shown here. A number of formulae which combine (monthly) rainfall and air temperature are available for this purpose.

The map reflects the south–north trend of air temperatures as well as the east–west and altitudinal trend in rainfall and raindays. The most southerly peninsulas of Cork and Kerry have more than 250 grazing days in the season while much of low-lying Munster and Leinster are rated between 225 and 250 days. The more elevated and wetter parts of Munster and Leinster as well as much of Ulster and Connaght have ratings of 200–235 days.

The formula used only considers temperature and rainfall, and takes no account of local soil properties. The low values shown for the highlands of north Co. Clare are probably incorrect, as the excellent drainage and extensive rock outcrop in the limestone areas give an unusually extended grazing season where herbage is available.

Keane, T., 1988. Features of the Irish climate of importance to agriculture: comparison with neighbouring Europe, in: Proceedings of Conference on Weather and Climate, edited by T. Keane. Agmet Group, Dublin.
Smith, L.P., 1976. The Agricultural Climate of England and Wales. Technical Bulletin 35, Ministry of Agriculture, Fisheries and Food. Her Majesty's Stationery Office, London.

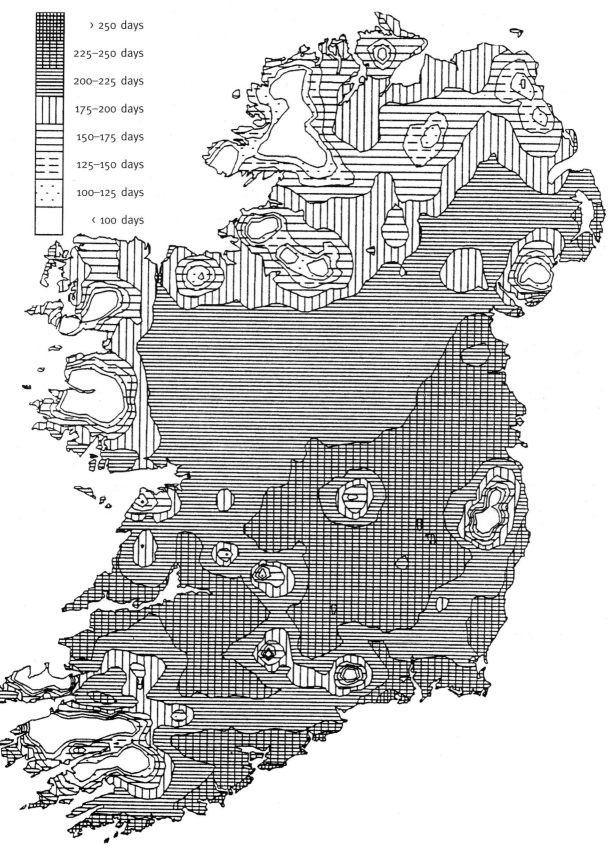

	› 250 days
	225–250 days
	200–225 days
	175–200 days
	150–175 days
	125–150 days
	100–125 days
	‹ 100 days

Mean length of grazing season (days/year), 1950–1980, based on the Smith Formula [number of days = 29.3T – 0.1R + 19.5, where T = mean annual air temperature, °C, and R = mean annual rainfall, mm/year]

A degree-day accumulation known as Ontario heat units was developed in Canada to estimate the growth maturity of corn (maize). The method takes into acount the daily maximum and minimum temperatures separately. The system uses two relationships, one for daytime temperature and another for night–time. The daytime relationship has a 10°C base and a curvilinear response to temperature (as the daily maximum temperature becomes higher above the threshold, the response to temperature is gradually slowed). The threshold for night-time temperature is 4.4°C and the response above that value is linear. The following table shows the comparison between ordinary degree-day accumations using base 10°C, starting on May 1st at Kilkenny in an average year:

	June 28	August 2	September 6	October 25
Degree-days above 10°C	170	353	566	683
Ontario heat units	685	1286	1874	2398

It has been estimated in England that a minimum of 628 degree-days were needed to produce maize at 24% dry matter and that locations with an average of 730 degree-days above base 10°C could probably produce silage maize of 24% dry matter nine years out of ten. Maize needs a minimum of 2400–2500 Ontario heat units in this period to produce an economical grain crop with 30% dry matter. Map (a) shows that this value is reached in the average year (may be taken as 5 years in 10) in Ireland. Map (b) indicates that if the grower desires to meet the criterion of 9 years in 10, Ontario heat units failed to reach this value.

Parameters such as Ontario heat units will be necessary to assess the suitability of certain locations in Ireland for new crops or of specific favourable locations for crops for early harvesting. Growers however should be particularly wary of predictions based on short-term temperature data.

Fitzgerald, D., 1992. Climatological data archive of the Irish Meteorological Service—an agricultural resource? In: Future of Irish Agriculture—Role of Climate, edited by J.F. Collins. Proceedings of 1992 Agmet conference, Dublin.

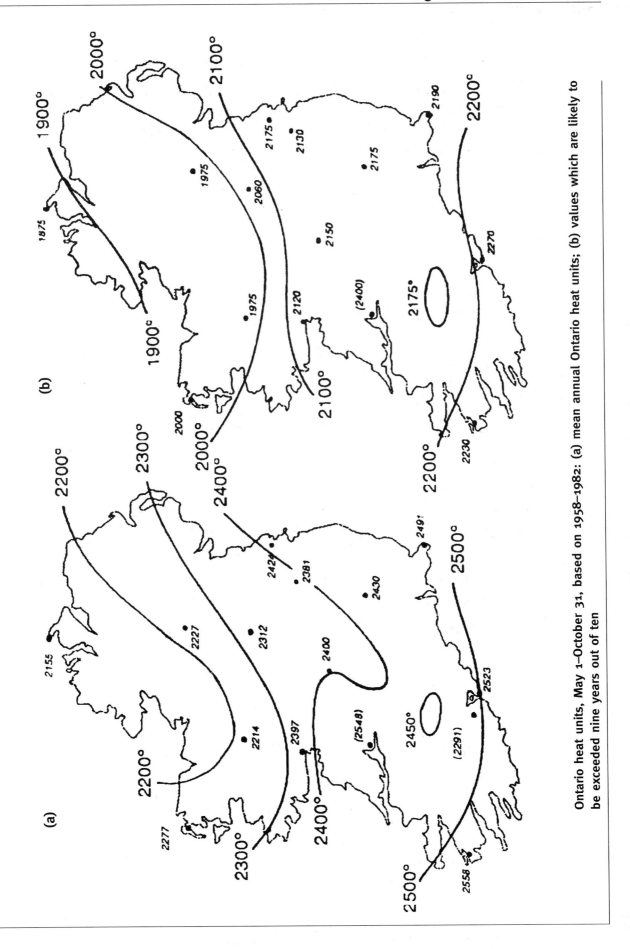

Ontario heat units, May 1–October 31, based on 1958–1982: (a) mean annual Ontario heat units; (b) values which are likely to be exceeded nine years out of ten

Suitability for tillage and grassland

Map (a) shows a simple version of a tillage suitability classification while map (b) depicts grazing potential. In creating these maps many aspects of climate and soil were taken into account, chiefly wetness, droughtiness, liability of flooding, altitude, exposure and trafficability, earliness of growth based on temperature, and likelihood of frosts.

Map (a) places the land of the country into five categories of suitability ranging from "highly suitable" to "unsuitable" for tillage. The highly suitable land is confined to parts of the provinces of Leinster and Munster which are generally the driest, the warmest, have an early spring, and have long periods drier than field capacity, giving plenty of opportunities for ripening and harvesting. The "suitable" class includes areas that are wetter (or, in some cases, more droughty), and with fewer degree-days and sunshine hours.

The unsuitable areas are mountainous, peaty, wet or have some other permanent limitation to tillage operations or crops. In some limited circumstances, reclamation of these areas for tillage may be possible, but the costs involved and the subsequent difficulties in crop production, combined with at least some availability of more suitable land, rules out their use for tillage.

Map (b) shows that the pasture grass swards are less demanding than most tillage crops, and hence up to half of the country including large parts of all four provinces, and parts of almost all counties, have soils and land in the best ("high") category for grazing. The "low" category includes mountain and hill pastures which have a low capacity due mainly to limitations of soil, high rainfall and low evapotranspiration. The unclassified category includes reclaimed peat soils both in the midlands and the west. These are a special case—they vary a lot depending on artificial drainage, and have local problems such as nutritional deficiencies.

Barry, P., 1986. Potential of the Irish Climate for Agriculture. Chapter 13 in: Climate Weather and Irish Agriculture, edited by T. Keane. Agmet Group, Dublin.

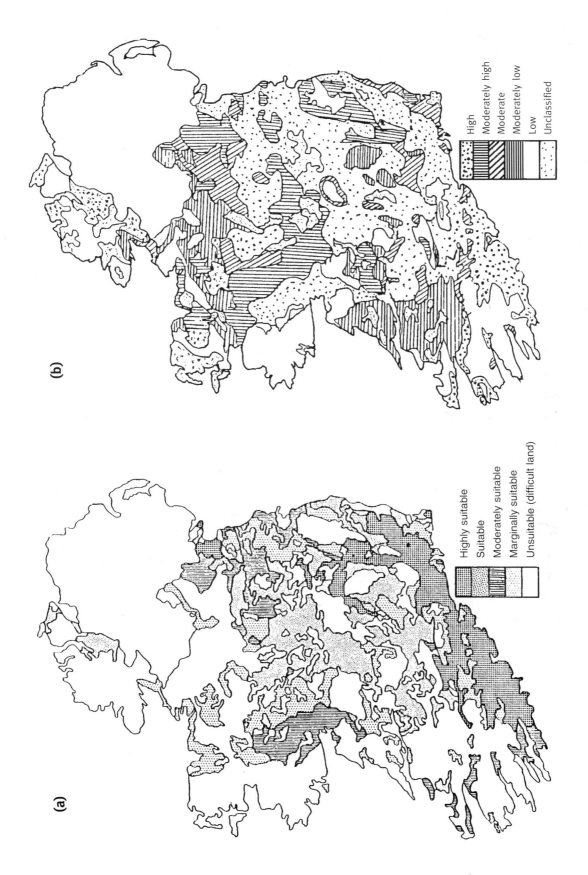

(b)

High
Moderately high
Moderate
Moderately low
Low
Unclassified

(a)

Highly suitable
Suitable
Moderately suitable
Marginally suitable
Unsuitable (difficult land)

Suitability for (a) tillage and (b) grassland

Herbage losses due to drought

It takes the occasional very dry and warm summer such as 1995 to convince most people that yields of grass in Ireland may be limited by drought. However actual measurement of soil moisture deficits or the calculation of water budgets using precipitation and evapotranspiration data will indicate that soils can and do become droughty and may benefit from irrigation. These maps show the regional distribution of dry matter yield loss in pastures at a standard rate of nitrogen application (250 kg/ha), based on Meteorological Service records and experimental data. Average calculated losses for the period 1956–1975 are shown in map (a), maximum losses in the five driest years in (b), minimum losses in the five driest years in (c) and maximum losses in the five wettest years in (d).

In general, yield losses are greatest in the south–east coastal areas and diminish towards the north–west. Losses are also greater in most coastal areas than inland, as a result of greater evaporative losses of water in the more windy conditions of coastal areas. On average, the southeast–northwest trend of loss of production ranges from zero to 1.4 tonnes of dry matter per hectare, but in the five driest years in twenty, the losses are in the region of 1.5 to 4 tons. The loss of grass dry matter with increasing altitude above 100 m would be about 0.5 ton/ha annually in the eastern and southern regions and 0.2 tons/ha per year in the western regions for each 100 m of increase in altitude.

Maps of this scale fail to show local differences arising from soil type, aspect, meso-climate and a range of managerial decisions affecting production of grass. While it is unlikely that individual farmers will ever find it economical to irrigate grassland, information such as this alerts them to the need to plan alternative strategies for dry years.

Brereton, A.J. and Keane, T., 1982. The effects of water on grass productivity in Ireland. Irish Journal of Agricultural Research 21: 227–248.
Brereton, A.J., Jones, M.B. and Burke, J.I., 1986. Weather and Crop Production. Chapter 7 in: Climate, Weather and Irish Agriculture, edited by T. Keane. Agmet Group, Dublin.

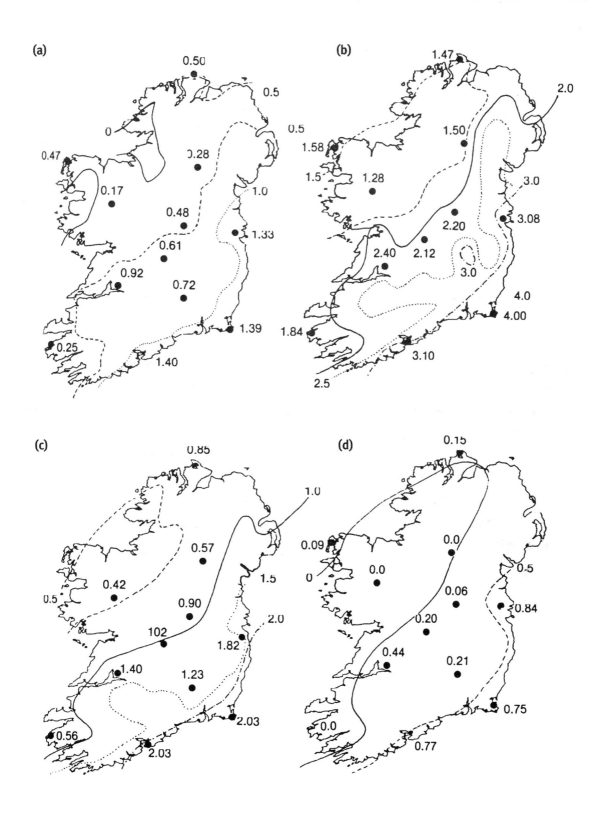

Annual herbage dry matter losses due to drought, tonnes per hectare, 1956–1975:
(a) average losses; (b) maximum losses in the five driest years; (c) minimum losses in the
five driest years; (d) maximum losses in the five wettest years

Grazing capacity of soil series in Laois

In this map, soil series with similar capability for the growth, management and use of grass are grouped together into categories identified by numerals 2 to 9. The parameter used is livestock units per hundred hectares (LU/100 ha), and two ranges are given, one for a low level of applied nitrogen fertilizer (48 kg/(ha year)) and one for a much higher rate (230 kg/(ha year)). The higher rates are considered only for classes 2 to 6; the remaining classes, 7, 8 & 9, consist of land unsuitable for intensive grass production due to wetness, exposure, limiting soil properties such as steep slopes, rock outcrop, shallowness, poor permeability, flood hazard or others.

Soil series in grazing capacity class 2 are generally well drained, medium-textured brown earth and grey-brown podzolic soils, while those in Class 3 may have some wetness or drought limitations. While the Stradbally Series is placed in Class 2, its Rocky Phase is in Class 3. The accurate placement of organic and alluvial soils is difficult since large variations in soil properties occur over short distances (they are mapped as complexes rather than as soil series) and grazing capacity classes from 3 to 6 may occur in the same field. In the case of peat soils, one has to balance a very high yield in mid summer (when water-holding capacity is a great attribute) against restricted grazing in spring and autumn due to poor trafficability.

It is to be emphasised that this classification is of grazing capacity for optimum agricultural productivity. A completely diferent ordering system would be used for other land uses such as suitability for wildlife, or for leisure pursuits.

Conry, M.J., 1989. Soils of Co. Laois. Soil Survey Bulletin No. 41. An Foras Talúntais, Dublin.
Diamond S., Teagasc, Johnstown Castle.

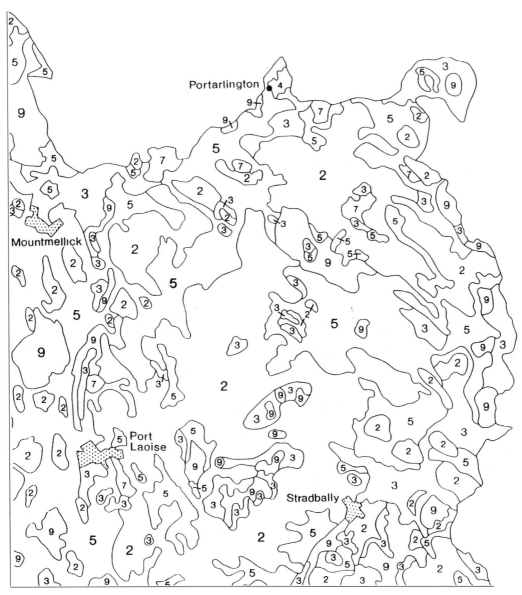

L.U./100 ha		Grazing capacity class
48kg N/ha	230kg N/ha	
210-222	264-276	2
197-210	252-264	3
185-197	227-252	4
173-185	202-227	5
160-173	188-202	6
148-160	—	7
135-148	—	8
‹135	—	9

Grazing capacity (livestock units per hundred hectares) and grazing capacity class of soil series in part of Co. Laois, at two rates of nitrogen application

Climate, blight and famine

It has been fairly well established that the dampness and dullness of the Irish climate makes it more suitable to the production of a tuber crop like the potato than to that of cereal crops such as wheat and oats. These climatological factors and associated high incidence of wetness, warm temperatures and high relative humidity are also conducive to the proliferation of the fungus which causes the disease of blight, namely *Phytophthora infestans*. It is not surprising therefore that, given the vast acreage of potatoes grown in nineteenth-century Ireland to feed a rapidly increasing population, disease outbreaks were common. The worst outbreaks occurred in 1846 and 1847 as a result of combinations of temperature, humidity and wind conditions, which favoured the spread of *Phytophthora infestans* and reduced the green photosynthesising crop to a rotting mass.

The outbreak has been traced back to 1845 when it first appeared in Flanders near the end of June; by mid-July it had spread to northern France and the Netherlands; frequent spells of warm easterly and southeasterly winds spread the spores across the Channel to England; it extended northwards during August and by mid September, parts of Ireland and Scotland were affected. By the end of October all of Ireland was affected (map (a)). The combination of three wet summers, the total reliance by the masses on this single crop, and social conditions which prevented their access to the other (plentiful) food crops, led catastrophically to hunger, disease, starvation and death.

Because of the late arrival of the fungus, towards the end of the summer, much of the 1845 crop was saved, but the spores overwintered, ensuring that the 1846 crop was infected early. Only a single variety of potato was generally grown—the Lumper; very high-yielding, but very susceptible to blight and now no longer grown—and this contributed to the spread of the disease.

Map (b) shows meteorologic conditions favourable to potato blight. On the morning indicated, a combination of maritime tropical air (mT) and a frontal rain belt were set to produce ideal conditions for the infection and spread of the fungus.

Bourke, A., 1987. Half a lifetime with potato blight, in: The Irish Meteorological Service The First Fifty Years 1936–1986, edited by L. Shields. The Stationery Office, Dublin.

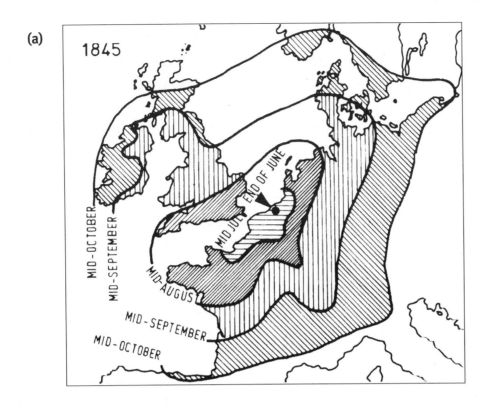

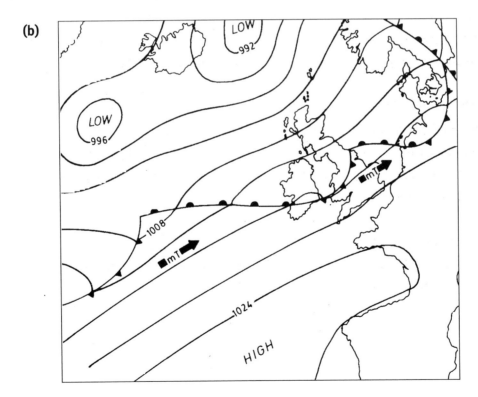

Climate, blight and famine: (a) the spread of the potato blight fungus, *Phytophthora infestans*, during the summer of 1845; (b) synoptic chart of conditions suited to the spread of blight (mT is maritime tropical air)

Liver fluke and potato blight

A major contribution of climatology to Irish agriculture is the ability to relate the incidence of plant and animal diseases to climatic conditions. When this knowledge is coupled with plant and animal physiology and pathology, measures can be taken to reduce the causes and the consequences of several diseases. The best known cases where forecasts and susceptibility ratings have proved very useful pertain to potato blight and liver fluke.

Liver fluke is a disease of cattle and sheep due to a parasite (a flatworm, *Fasciola hepatica*) whose existence and life cycle depend on a terrestrial snail (*Lymnaea trunculata*) which proliferates in wet soils. While temperature is important at early (young) stages, water is essential to the parasite's survival and hence the incidence of the disease is lowest in the drier southern and eastern part of the country, especially on well-drained soils. The susceptibility increases in a northwesterly direction, reaching a maximum in the high-rainfall, bog-blanketed landscape of west Mayo. The numbers 350, 400 and 450 on map (a) refer to a prediction model (Ollerenshaw index) which is based on monthly values for precipitation, wet days and potential evapotranspiration.

Susceptibility to potato blight is based on an accumulation of effective blight hours (EBH) which in turn are based on computations involving periods of time with air temperature over 10°C, a relative humidity above 90%, and the maintenance of a film of water on the potato plant leaves for a suitable period. Map (b) shows that blight weather is a most serious risk along the warmer, humid south coast (>400 EBH) while the risk declines inland and northward with decreasing night-time temperatures.

Warnings of weather likely to be conducive to the spread of blight are issued most years in June–August, together with advice as to opportunities suitable for spraying (a short dry spell that would allow the spray to dry on the leaves). In the high-incidence areas of the south, routine spraying may be necessary where large crop areas are involved.

O'Reilly, G., 1988. Environmental aspects of Irish climate, in: Proceedings of Conference on Weather and Agriculture, edited by T. Keane. Agmet Group, Dublin.
Hope Cawdery, M.J., 1988. Weather, animal disease and modelling, in : Proceedings of Conference on Weather and Agriculture, edited by T. Keane. Agmet Group, Dublin.

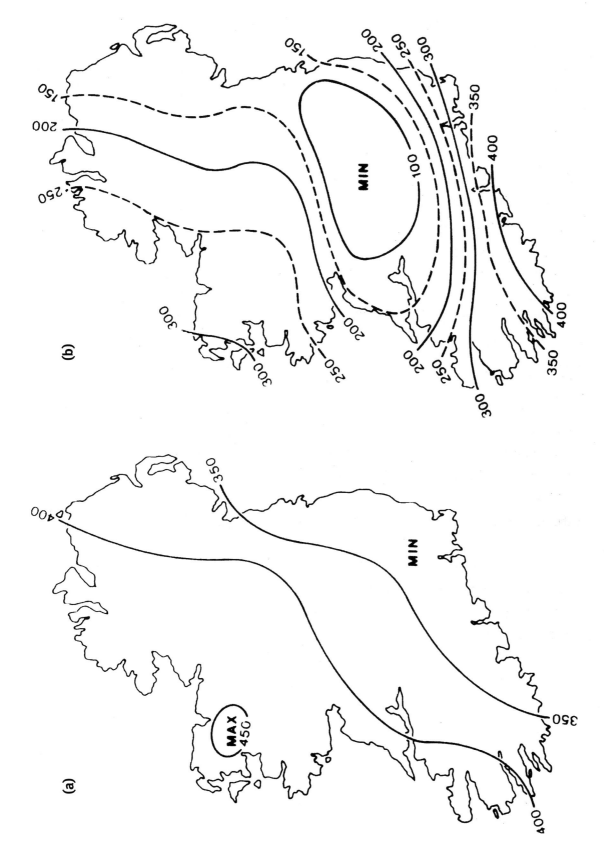

Liver fluke and potato blight: (a) annual Ollerenshaw indices; (b) mean annual cumulative effective blight hours

Valuation of land

From time immemorial, governments, monarchs, conquerors and rulers have made attempts to put a monetary value on land with a view to collecting taxes. Prior to the middle of the last century a number of diverse schemes existed in the various baronies and counties of Ireland and were singularly uneven in the amount of tax demanded; they varied a thousand-fold on an acreage basis in some instances. With the establishment of the Poor Law Unions a standard system of levying tax on property was devised. The valuation was carried out under the direction of Richard Griffith and became known as the Griffith Valuation. The 6-inch to 1 mile maps were coming on stream at the time (1830–1850) and each townland was divided into a number of lots depending on its size and intensity of use. The value placed on each lot was based on soil properties, land use and proximity to towns and markets; it varied from a few pence per acre for the poorest of boggy and rocky land to about £1.5.0 per acre (£3.08 per hectare) for the best of land near towns and cities. Initially the valuation which was arrived at referred to individual townlands and was aggregated and published according to civil parish, barony and county. Subsequently a new act was passed in 1852, which stated that every tenement or rateable hereditament was to be separately valued, the valuation of land being made on an estimate of its net annual value having regard to the general average prices in forty Irish market towns during the years 1849, 1850 and 1851 of certain staple articles of agricultural value.

The effects of the Irish climate and soil types are reflected in the national picture for land values. Land north and west of a line from the south coast of Cork to the north coast of Antrim is much less valuable than land to the east. Most of the wet and boggy land and the steep and rocky land is situated in the north and west. Good quality land dominates Leinster, East Munster and East Ulster even though in the latter province values reflected the prosperity associated with the linen industry.

The Griffith valuation continued as a basis for collecting taxes (Rates) until 1923 in Northern Ireland and until 1982 in the rest of the island. Anomalously low values assigned to excellent land in Co. Wexford eventually brought the system into disrepute.

Johnson, J.J., 1970. The Two "Irelands" at the beginning of the nineteenth century. Chapter 14 in: Irish Geographical Studies, edited by N. Stephens and R.E. Glasscock. The Queen's Univeristy, Belfast.

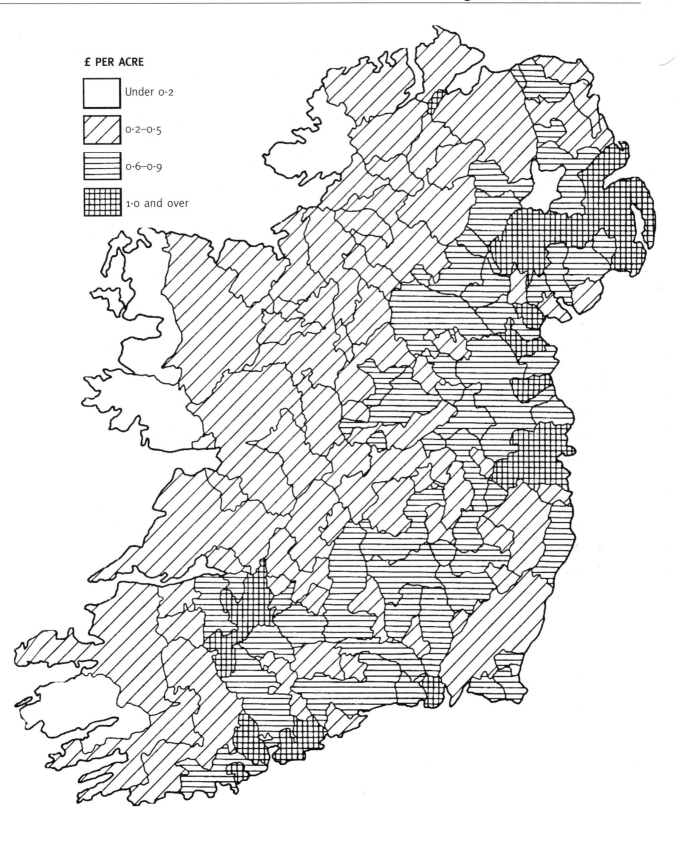

£ PER ACRE

- Under 0·2
- 0·2–0·5
- 0·6–0·9
- 1·0 and over

Valuation of rural areas, £/acre, about 1850, based on the Griffith Valuation

Valuation of land in Co. Cork

A better relationship between the properties and characteristics of land and the rateable valuation assigned to it under the Primary (Griffith) Valuation is seen at county level. This map for Co. Cork is an example. Due to a wide variation in topography, climatology, infrastructure, communications, etc. the value assigned varied from the lowest to the highest.

At a general level, the mountainous areas have the lowest values while lands close to Cork city have the highest. Land along the mountains bordering Co. Kerry, and along the central east-west spine of the Boggeragh/Nagle mountains, have a combination of limitations many of which are climatic. These areas generally have high rainfall and humidity, low evaporation, fewer degree-days and lower sunshine hours and radiation receipts. In the eastern and less elevated areas the land is more suitable for a wide range of crops, growing and grazing seasons are longer and harvesting is easier. Another climatic influence on the valuation may be gleaned from the moderately high values assigned to land along the south coast, reflecting the moderating influences of the sea on local temperatures.

Proximity to markets (towns and ports) was also a criterion used in assigning a value to land, and the positions of Cork city and most of the major towns can be easily seen from the values given to land around them. (The positions of Skibbereen and Macroom are not immediately obvious—probably a legacy of the 1840's Famine which was especially severe in these areas).

Smyth, W.J., 1993. Social, Economic and Landscape Transformations in County Cork from the Mid-eighteenth to the Mid-nineteenth Century. Chapter 16 in: Cork—History and Society, edited by P. O'Flanagan and C.G. Buttimer. Geography Publications, Dublin.

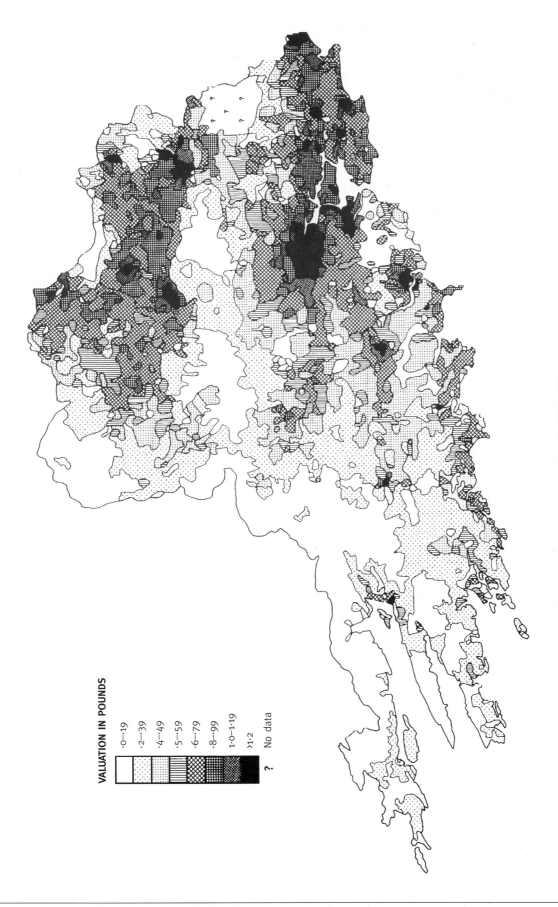

VALUATION IN POUNDS

- ·0—·19
- ·2—·39
- ·4—·49
- ·5—·59
- ·6—·79
- ·8—·99
- 1·0—1·19
- >1·2
- No data
- ?

Valuation of land in Co. Cork, £/acre, in 1851, based on the Griffith Valuation

Risk of water pollution from septic tank systems

Ever since they were patented over 100 years ago, septic tank systems have been used in increasing numbers in rural areas to treat waste matter. There are now over 300,000 septic tank systems serving a population of about 1.2 million people in Ireland. The amount of water passing through these is enormous—50 million gallons per day or 80 million cubic metres annually. This effluent poses a risk to groundwater and hence the choice of a percolation area is critical since it is in the ground that the main treatment takes place. The soil and subsoil act as filtering, absorbing and ion-exchanging mechanisms in which the contaminants such as nitrogen and phosphorus, various salts, bacteria and viruses are removed. It is essential to have a suitable kind and sufficient thickness of soil and subsoil. The ideal thickness is a minimum of 3 m over the groundwater surface or rock, and the ideal soil is a fairly fine-textured one with moderate permeability. If it is too permeable, the contaminated water will flow through it too quickly; if it is too impermeable, the water stays on the surface. The ideal underlying rock is a porous, granular one (not a fissured one).

This map shows that up to 60% of the country has a medium or high risk of pollution to surface or groundwater from septic tanks. The peaty, hilly and mountainous areas are risky since they have watertable at or near the surface, or have bare rock or very shallow soil. Parts of Mayo, Galway and Clare, as well as shallow valleys scattered around the country, pose a high risk to groundwater since the soil is thin and the rock underneath is fissured (karstic limestone). Likewise, parts of most counties have areas of gravelly sandy soils (too permeable) or shallow soils, steep slopes, and wet soils which are not ideal percolating areas for waste water. The rest of the country is farily "safe" but care must be taken since soils vary from place to place even within single fields.

Daly, D., 1995, private communication. Geological Survey of Ireland, Dublin.
Daly, D., Thorn, R. and Henry, H., 1993. Septic Tank Systems and Groundwater in Ireland. Report 93/1, Geological Survey of Ireland, Dublin.

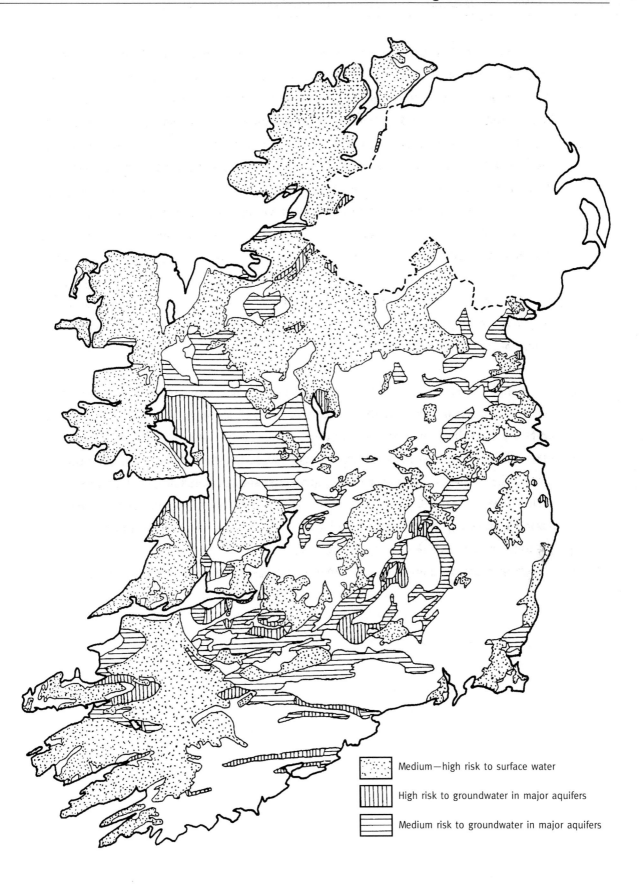

	Medium—high risk to surface water
	High risk to groundwater in major aquifers
	Medium risk to groundwater in major aquifers

Risk of water pollution from septic tank systems

Winter rainfall acceptance potential of soils

Winter rainfall acceptance is a concept of interest to all those who use land in the wet winter months. They include those who outwinter livestock, plant winter cereals, harvest out-of-season crops such as sugar beet, and those who want to use suitable opportunities to carry out other operations in the winter such as disposal of farm wastes. The concept includes the interplay between soil, site and climate; soil characteristics used to draw up categories of winter rainfall acceptance include drainable porosity, infiltration capacity and hydraulic conductivity. Site characteristics are expressed in terms of angle and length of slopes, while the chief climatic parameters are mean date of return to field capacity, mean monthly (winter) rainfall and potential evapotranspiration.

This map shows the country divided into four classes of winter rain acceptance potential. All the well-drained brown earth, brown podzolic, grey-brown podzolic and reclaimed podzol soils are placed in the "very high and high" category, which dominates the southeastern half of the country. The "moderate" category land is at higher altitudes, on steeper slopes, and in higher rainfall areas and has a more westerly and northerly distribution pattern. It includes some gleys, as well as shallow and heavier soils in the eastern half of the country. Land in the "low and very low" category includes the great expanses of gleys in the "drumlin belt" and on the shale plateaux of the Clare/Kerry/Limerick area, as well as shallow soils. The "unclassified" land incudes both the raised and blanket peats, bare rock and steep mountain slopes, which generally have extremely low acceptance potentials.

As with most simplified maps, each category contains land of a wide range of properties, and each particular site should be judged by reference to published data on climate and soils, and examination of the site itself.

Gardiner, M.J., 1986. Use of soil and climatic data to predict hydraulic loading behaviour of Irish soils. Soil Use and Management 2 (4): 146–149.

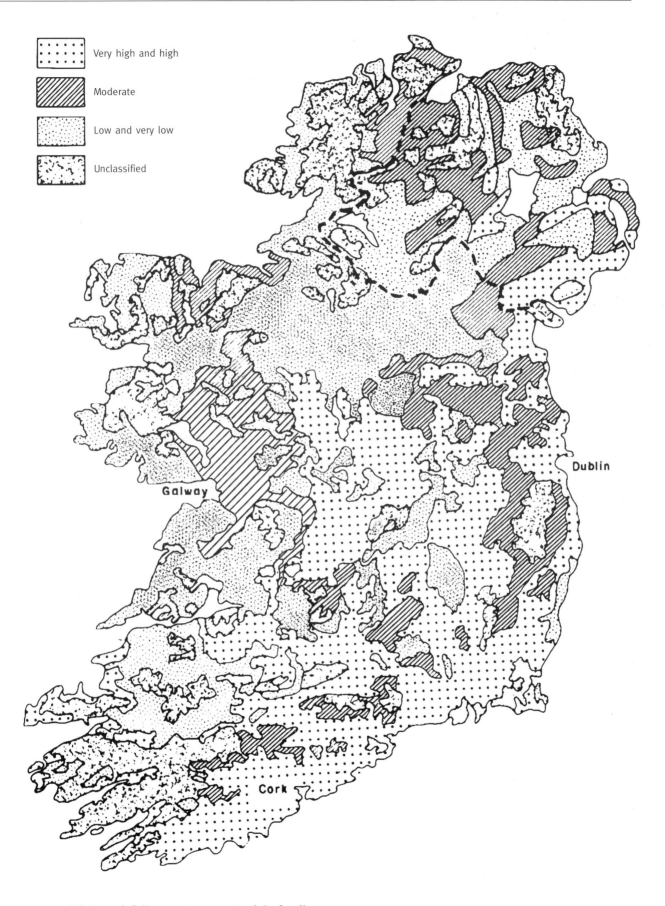

Very high and high

Moderate

Low and very low

Unclassified

Galway

Dublin

Cork

Winter rainfall acceptance potential of soils

Provisional windzones for forestry

This map shows windzones for forestry in Britain, and provisional windzones for Ireland. The windzones are based on the use of tatter flags as a method of measuring exposure. In a tatter flag survey, standardised unhemmed cotton flags are deployed throughout an area, across a range of altitudes. The rate at which material is lost from the fraying edge of the flag is an empirical measure of exposure, and depends in complicated ways on wind speeds, precipitation and frost. During the survey, flags are periodically replaced, and the mean tatter rate over a three-year period is taken. The tatter-flag method of measuring exposure was first used to quantify local exposure, to choose a site for a house on the Orkney Islands. Regionally, tatter flag information has contributed significantly to the prediction of limiting exposure for commercial forest productivity and for wind-damage risk assessment for forestry.

The rate of flag tatter increases with altitude, but the rate of the increase varies regionally. Within each windzone mapped, there is a constant rate of increase in flag tatter with altitude. In the windier areas (zones A, B), the rate of increase in flag tatter with altitude is faster than in the less windy areas (zones E, F). The zones shown for Britain are based on extensive tatter-flag surveys over several decades. For Ireland, this is only a first approximation, based on limited tatter flag information for Northern Ireland only, and on published maps of windspeed (page 129). Experience suggests that the Irish zones are biased towards the southwest, and that the northwest extremities of the island should be shown as windzone A, with only the peninsulas in this zone in Munster.

Miller, K.F., 1986. Windthrow hazard in conifer plantations. Irish Forestry 43 (1): 66–78.
Miller, K.F., 1985. Windthrow Hazard Classification. Leaflet No. 85, Forestry Commission. Her Majesty's Stationery Office, London.

Provisional windzones for predicting windthrow hazard in conifer plantations, Britain and Ireland

Site types for forestry

Forest tree species differ widely in their site requirements, but exact specifications are not generally available. Moreover, the tendency for only the cheapest land to be planted has given rise to the impression that trees will grow productively on the least fertile and most poorly-drained land.

As with a great range of crops, trees generally grow best on moderately well-drained loamy soil with slightly acid reaction and a plentiful supply of nutrients. The only general restriction is that most conifers will not put their roots into soil with a pH above six.

The shallow limestone soils mapped here are not usually suited to conifers. These, and the gravel and sand soils are also restricted in their use for many trees by drought. Dry fertile mineral soils have the widest use range for forestry, as for most other agricultural enterprises, with which forestry must compete. Wetter and less fertile mineral soils give a wide variety of high-yielding forest crop opportunities, and offer some of the best options for commercial forestry. Where basin peat and alluvium can be drained, excellent sites for a wide range of species can be found, though late spring frosts (page 117) are a problem with some.

Wet mineral soils can give very high yields for Sitka spruce—some of the most productive timber stands in temperate latitudes are on Irish drumlin soils. Poor drainage restricts rooting, however, and in the more windy areas (page 129), and on high or exposed ground, the risk of windthrow losses is high.

Blanket peat and peaty soils usually support very few commercial forest tree species, and yields are not high. Despite low land prices, windthrow risk and harvesting difficulties mean that only very well-managed plantations are likely to be commercially viable on these sites.

Cummins, T. and Whelan, D.P., in praparation. Woodland Establishment and Management for the Timber Grower. Irish Timber Growers' Association, Dublin.
Gardiner, M.J. and Radford, T., 1980. Soil Asscoiations of Ireland and Their Land Use Potential. Soil Survey Bulletin No. 36. An Foras Talúntais, Dublin.

	Dry fertile mineral soils
	Wetter or less fertile mineral soils
	Wet mineral soils
	Blanket peat and peaty soils
	Basin peat and alluvium
	Soils on gravel and sand
	Shallow limestone soils
	Water and urban areas

Principal site types for afforestation, based on Soil Map of Ireland, 1980

Exceedence of critical load of acidity for soils

Heavy doses of acid rain or other pollutants can cause direct damage to vegetation. The main concern about the long-term effects of nitrogen and sulphur in the rain, however, is damage to soil by acidification. Because of the complex chemical systems in soils, it is usually possible for soils to accept significant quantities of acids without undergoing any net acidification. The maximum acceptable amount of acid input is called the critical load.

Soils are mapped here according to the current exceedence of their critical loads. This map is therefore a combination of a soil map, the precipitation map, and maps of the acids in precipitation (page 147). Those areas shown darkest have their soils' critical loads exceeded by the largest amount, and in these areas, active soil acidification due to acid precipitation is most likely to occur (though its identification on the ground is difficult).

The critical loads concept is best developed at present for mineral soils, and while many peat areas shown on this map in black have their critical loads exceeded, they are strongly acid environments in any case, and this may not be a problem. It is on the acid mineral soils in mountain regions adjoining the high-level blanket peat areas that soil acidification is most likely to be a potential problem. In these areas, the possible effects of soil acidification are on plant roots, restricting uptake of nutrients, and on fish in streams draining these areas.

Aherne, J.J. (private communication, 1995). Forest Ecosystem Research Group, University College, Dublin.

>1000

0–500

Not exceeded

Preliminary estimates of exceedence of critical load of acidity for soils, mol ha^{-1} year^{-1} above the maximum acceptable deposition of acids

Beaufort scale of wind forces

Beaufort Number	Short Description	Effects on land	Effects at sea	Wind speed at 10 m above land or sea level		
				Knots	m/s	miles/h
0	Calm	Smoke rises vertically	Glass-smooth sea	<1	<0.3	<1
1	Light Air	Direction of wind shown by smoke but not wind vanes	Surface disturbed	1–3	0.3–1.5	1–3
2	Light Breeze	Wind felt on face; leaves rustle, ordinary wind vanes moved by wind	Ripples and wavelets	4–6	1.6–3.3	4–7
3	Gentle Breeze	Leaves and small twigs in constant motion; wind extends a light flag	Cats' paws on surface; waves form	7–10	3.4–5.4	8–12
4	Moderate Breeze	Raises dust and loose paper; small branches are moved	Occasional white horses; limit of dinghy sailing	11–16	5.5–7.9	13–18
5	Fresh Breeze	Small trees in leaf begin to sway; crested wavelets form on inland waters	Frequent white horses, occasionally trailing	17–21	8.0–10.7	19–24
6	Strong Breeze	Large branches in motion; whistling heard in telegraph wires; umbrellas used with difficulty	Trailing white crests to waves; spray noticeable; decked day-cruising yachts restricted	22–27	10.8–13.8	25–31
7	Near Gale	Whole trees in motion; inconvenience felt when walking against the wind	Long trails of foam; occasional waves above horizon	28–33	13.9–17.1	32–38
8	Gale	Breaks twigs off trees; generally impedes progress; trees uprooted on susceptible sites; driving occasionally unsteady	Large breaking waves; spray affects visibility; frequent waves over horizon; small trawlers restricted	34–40	17.2–20.7	39–46
9	Strong Gale	Slight structural damage occurs (chimney pots and slates removed); large branches fall off big trees.	Sea mostly white with foam; visibility much reduced; horizon occasionally obscured	41–47	20.8–24.4	47–54
10	Storm	Seldom experienced inland; many trees uprooted; considerable structural damage occurs	Sea completely broken into crests and foam; Large vessels impeded, ferries delayed	58–55	24.5–28.4	55–63
11	Violent Storm	Very rarely experienced; accompanied by widespread damage; healthy trees uprooted; road travel seriously restricted	Mountainous seas; horizon regularly obscured; visibility drastically reduced, all shipping affected	56–63	28.5–32.6	64–72
12	Hurricane	Widespread destruction	Major damage to windward coasts; shipping stopped	>64	>32.7	>73

Bord Iascaigh Mhara,
Crofton Road,
Dunlaoghaire,   (01) 284 1544
Co. Dublin.   (01) 284 1123 fax

Environmental Protection Agency,
Ardcavan,   (053) 47120
Wexford.   (053) 47119 fax

St. Martin's House,
Waterloo Road,   (01) 660 2511
Dublin 4.   (01) 668 0009 fax

Geological Survey of Ireland,
Beggar's Bush,   (01) 670 7444
Dublin 4.   (01) 668 1782 fax

Geological Survey of Northern Ireland,
20 College Gardens,   (01232) 666 595
Belfast BT9 6BS.   (01232) 662 835 fax

Meteorological Service,
Glasnevin,   (01) 842 4411
Dublin 9.   (01) 837 5557 fax

Weather Forecasts   (01) 842 5555
                        (01)842 4655
Climatological Enquiries (01) 837 5436

Meteorological Office Northern Ireland,
1 College Square East, (01232) 328 457
Belfast BT1 6BQ.   (01232) 328 457 fax

Office of Public Works,
Hydrometric Division,
17 Lower Hatch Street,   (01) 661 3111
Dublin 2.   (01) 676 1714 fax

Ordnance Survey Office,
Phoenix Park,
Dublin 8.   (01) 820 6100
Map Sales   (01) 820 6439
                        (01) 820 6443
                        (01) 820 4156 fax

Ordnance Survey of Northern Ireland,
Colby House,
Stranmillis Court,   (01232) 661 244
Belfast BT9 5BJ.   (01232) 683 211 fax

St. Mary's College of Education,
Falls Road,   (01232) 671 631
Belfast.   (01232) 624 166 fax

Teagasc (formerly An Foras Talúntais),

Agriculture and Food Development Authority,

19 Sandymount Avenue,	(01) 668 8188
Dublin 4.	(01) 668 8023 fax
Athenry,	(091) 844 473
Co. Galway.	(091) 844 296 fax
Ballyhaise,	(049) 38300
Co. Cavan.	(049) 38304 fax
Grange,	
Dunsany,	(046) 25214
Co. Meath.	(046) 26154 fax
Johnstown Castle,	(053) 42888
Wexford.	(053) 43004 fax
Kinsealy,	
Malahide Road,	(01) 846 0644
Dublin 17.	(01) 846 0524 fax
Oak Park,	(0503) 70200
Carlow.	(0503) 42423 fax
Moore Park,	
Fermoy,	(025) 31422
Co. Cork.	(025) 32563 fax
Piltown,	(056) 643 105
Co. Kilkenny.	(056) 643 446 fax

Trinity College, Dublin,

Botany Department,	(01) 608 1274
Dublin 2.	(01) 608 1147 fax
Environmental Science Unit	(01) 608 1638
	(01) 671 8047 fax
Department of Zoology	(01) 608 1366
	(01) 671 8047 fax

University College Dublin,

Department of Crop Science,	
Horticulture and Forestry,	
Belfield,	(01) 269 3244
Dublin 4.	(01) 706 1104 fax
Department of Environmental	
Resource Management,	
Belfield,	(01) 706 7737
Dublin 4.	(01) 706 1102 fax